For Dad — who introduced me
to the magic of wandering byways.

Acknowledgements

Backroad journeys are always more enjoyable with good companions. For the first edition of this volume I was accompanied by Rochelle Farquhar and my brother Don, both of whom assisted with navigation and driving. Don's help was particularly welcome when we bogged down in mud. Richard Jr. and Raven, my two sons, came along on most of the trips, making their own special contributions to our explorations.

During this revision I was accompanied by my father, Thomas Wright. His company made each of the roads special; we shared not only thoughts, dreams, jokes and ideas but the hard work and elation of pulling the van back onto the road. In fact he became so enamored with the country that a month later he returned for his own explorations.

Special thanks go to Sue Safaryn, who keyboarded the manuscript with precision, and editor David Dunsmuir, who watched over spelling and syntax as well as the design and laborious production details of the book with good humor.

Finally, hearty thanks to the good folks at Redhawk Rentals who graciously loaned me a 4x4 to complete the driving when my van shuddered at the thought of another backroad. Their support is much appreciated.

Contents

For the dedicated backroader, there's always another mountain beyond the mountain and another road to be explored.

What is a Backroad?

Backroads, byways, trails, tracks, cowpaths. Ask any 10 people what constitutes a backroad and you'll get as many different answers and definitions. To me a backroad is an unpaved route that leads slowly, but infallibly, through back-country to varying points of interest. It may be close to major centres of population, or far removed. It may be a wide, easy forest access road, or a narrow, steep and deeply rutted four-wheel-drive track. The byway may course flat along a river valley, or climb to a forest lookout tower and alpine meadows. It may go somewhere, or nowhere. These are backroads.

Despite this variety, backroads have one thing in common - they change, seldom remaining the same from one season to another. We may have travelled a certain route in spring and found it soft and muddy; later it may freeze with the first cold of winter. A culvert can plug and flood the road, or a logging company can improve a mudhole by adding a culvert. Nature may modify a route with a slide, or completely block it for a year or more. Some routes are being constantly upgraded, with curves removed and grades lessened. Others may have the culverts torn up and trees dropped across them to discourage travel. These road changes are a part of the thrill of backroading, but they require certain precautions. These precautions are detailed in a "Backroading Equipment" appendix near the end of this book.

Introduction

Backroads of the Hope to Clinton area, the third of four volumes covering territory easily accessible from the Lower Mainland, traverse the Interior plateau country bordering the coastal mountains. The altitudinal variation in landscape makes fascinating exploring: from arid river valleys into canyon country; through pine forests and open grassland dotted with lakes; up steep mountain sides to alpine meadows. The recreational opportunities are equally diversified: canoeing, rafting, fishing and gold panning on waterways; hiking, hunting, horseback riding, cross-country skiing, rockhounding, and camping on the hills and valleys; and photography and nature study everywhere.

The roads in this book follow the route of Simon Fraser and the trails of cattlemen and prospectors, Indians and settlers. They lead to mountain lakes and rainbow trout and to alkali potholes speckled with waterfowl. There are cool meadows and river rapids, reaction ferries, abandoned mines, ranches, wildlife and solitude, all to explore and enjoy.

Travelling the sparsely settled plateau country, I find it easy to relate to the life style of the Indians who lived in villages along the Fraser River when Simon Fraser passed through. Keekwillie holes for their steam baths can be found where their winter dwellings once stood; fishing platforms still used today can be seen along the river; and root-digging grounds can be visited where as many as 1000 Indians would gather in early summer. The natural resources they used add pleasure to today's back-country excursions.

A side trip up the West Road from Lytton (see Volume 1 of this series) will take you across the Stein River.

The trips mention local points of interest as well as the road conditions, suggested routes, scenic areas, historical locations, fishing and hunting opportunities and natural history areas. I like to think of this book and others in the series as "a pointer in the right direction." You will make new discoveries as you travel the routes and hike the side trails, and that is as it should be. It is not my purpose to tell you all you might see; this would destroy the sense of exploration and discovery that is so much a part of travelling these routes. I hope that the roads themselves will lead you to areas you like and that beyond road's end you will continue to explore, by whatever means you choose.

As all who live in British Columbia are aware, times have changed since the first volume in this series came out in 1977. It costs us more money to reach the back country; many services previously expected from government agencies such as the Forest Service and Parks Branch are now waning. We can argue the necessity and good sense of such cutbacks from both sides. The point is they have been made and it is now up to users to take a stronger role in maintaining the land. Please make an effort not only to leave few tracks and take out your trash but to clean up after others.

This second edition has been retitled to reflect the extended area travelled and the additional routes, now totalling eight. All routes were driven in the spring and fall of 1985 and the distances recalculated. However, remember that roads will change and be sure to take adequate maps and equipment for any emergencies.

Richard Wright

How to use this book

The Junction Country is arranged in a similar fashion to other books of the Special Interest Publications 'Backroads' series with directions and details at each stage along the route. All routes that can be started from either end have reverse mileages. For example, the West Fraser Road can be started at either North Bend or Lytton, so reverse mileages are given — that is, mileages for both directins. On the other hand, you can travel the Nahatlatch Road only from east to west, so the mileages are given in one direction only.

In addition, to keep with the highways system change to metric in 1977, the directions are given in kilometres. However, many of us still think in the Imperial system and older vehicles still have miles on their odometers, so the book is not completely metric. The layout of figures in the route description is as follows:

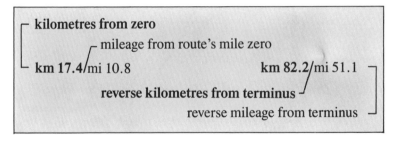

The difference between summer and winter tread can make a variation of one to two per cent, and a slippery hill may add a little as well. Keep this in mind and check your odometer against highway test sections and with known points in the description.

Appendices give information that may be of value and interest to backroaders. Despite the fact that they are at the back of the book it would be wise to read them before embarking on any of the various routes.

Finally, if you find errors or want to suggest subjects or areas for inclusion in other books of this series, please let me know through the publisher.

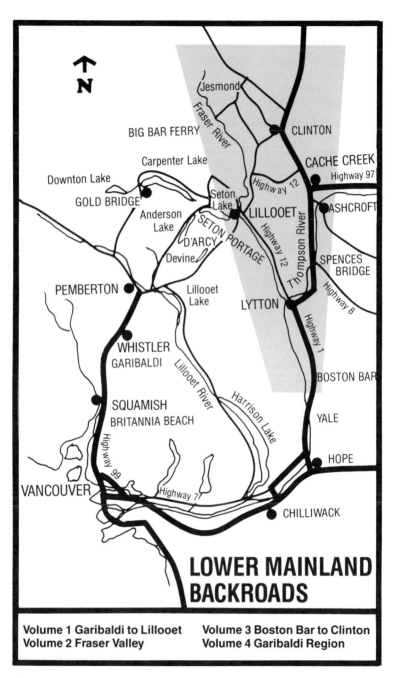

N

Jesmond

Fraser River

BIG BAR FERRY

Carpenter Lake

Downton Lake

GOLD BRIDGE

Anderson Lake

D'ARCY

Devine

Seton Lake

Seton Portage

CLINTON

CACHE CREEK

Highway 97

LILLOOET

ASHCROFT

Highway 12

Highway 12

Thompson River

SPENCES BRIDGE

PEMBERTON

Lillooet Lake

LYTTON

Highway 8

WHISTLER

GARIBALDI

Lillooet River

Harrison Lake

Highway 1

BOSTON BAR

SQUAMISH

BRITANNIA BEACH

YALE

Highway 99

HOPE

VANCOUVER

Highway 7

CHILLIWACK

LOWER MAINLAND
BACKROADS

Volume 1 Garibaldi to Lillooet   Volume 3 Boston Bar to Clinton
Volume 2 Fraser Valley   Volume 4 Garibaldi Region

Area introduction

The adjoining map shows the area covered by the 'Lower Mainland Backroads' series in four volumes. This book, Volume 3, includes the area around the canyon of the Fraser River up to Lytton, and the wedge of land between the Fraser and Thompson rivers north of Lytton and south of the Cariboo. The region is easily reached by those living in the Lower Mainland and most roads can be travelled by standard vehicles.

At least one of the routes detailed is a paved road (Highway 12) for its full length. It has been included because it provides access to other routes and in comparison to the more frequently travelled Cariboo Highway it is at least a byway if not a true backroad. Another road detailed is the Jesmond-Big Bar Road with side roads to Jesmond Lookout, Big Bar Mountain, Devil's Garden and Little White Lake, all of which begin along the Jesmond-Big Bar section. Other routes follow old trails and river valleys.

Junction Country backroads link up with routes in the 'Lower Mainland Backroads' series. For example, they meet routes from Volume 1, *Bridge River Country*, at Lytton, Lillooet and Big Bar. Volume 2 covers roads south and west of Volume 3; Volume 4 details connecting roads in the Fraser Valley. Combining all four volumes will make several circular routes available, using the Fraser Valley-Fraser Canyon going one way to the Interior, and the mountain passes north of Garibaldi going the other way. Big Bar can be reached in at least three ways, and both sides of the Fraser can be followed in some sections, using bridges and ferries for the crossings. In total, more than 2200 kilometres are discussed in the four volumes.

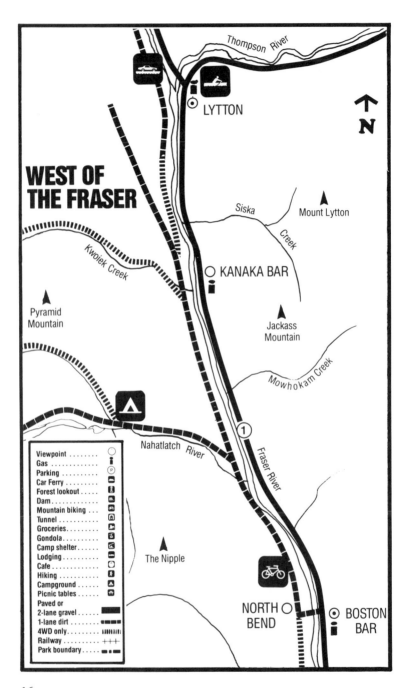

WEST OF
THE FRASER

Thompson River

LYTTON

Mount Lytton

Siska

Creek

Kwoiek Creek

KANAKA BAR

Pyramid
Mountain

Jackass
Mountain

Mowhokam Creek

Nahatlatch River

Fraser River

(1)

The Nipple

NORTH
BEND

BOSTON
BAR

Viewpoint	○
Gas	i
Parking	℗
Car Ferry	
Forest lookout	
Dam	
Mountain biking . . .	
Tunnel	
Groceries	
Gondola	
Camp shelter	
Lodging	
Cafe	
Hiking	
Campground	△
Picnic tables	
Paved or 2-lane gravel	▬▬▬
1-lane dirt	▬ ▬ ▬
4WD only	ⅠⅠⅠⅠⅠⅠ
Railway	+++
Park boundary	▬ ▬

Route One

West of the Fraser

Etched along the mountain on the west side of the Fraser, this road provides a new viewpoint for familiar Fraser Canyon landmarks. Eastward across the river the Trans-Canada Highway can be seen on the rock wall — wider and less perilous now, but still following the original Cariboo Wagon Road. Above the highway the slopes are drier and less treed than those west of the river; they reach to a plateau area, giving the country a different feeling. Below the road the railway tracks wind along the river course. The whole scene looks like a model railway set that stretches for miles, complete with moving trains and cars. The more traffic you see across the river, the more pleased you can feel about taking the less travelled route.

The west-side road provides access to other backroads and recreation areas. A logging road into the Nahatlatch Valley offers fishing along the river, canoeing on its lakes and camping at several Forest Service Recreation sites. Details of the route are contained in this volume. At the north end of the North Bend to Lytton route, the road continues west of the Fraser from Lytton to Lillooet, a backroad covered in Volume 1 of the series.

Access to the west-side road is by bridge at Boston Bar and a reaction ferry at Lytton. The reaction ferry, an unusual form of transport, seems a relic of former days; even more interesting was the aerial ferry which operated at Boston Bar until early 1986. The cagelike, one-car ferry was built in 1940 and for 46 years swung commuters across the 243-metre span of the river in 90 seconds. The ferry was usually about 35 metres above the river but in the flood of 1948 it cleared by only one metre. Although the aerial ferry was stalled in mid-swing by power failures on occasion it was a great improvement over the rowboat ferry that it replaced. If North Bend residents have their way the old cage will be in the town as a tourist attraction.

The ferry has been replaced with the Cog Harrington Bridge, named for Walter Cog Harrington, a pioneer Fraser Canyon trucker and advocate who died in 1980 at the age of 66. While the bridge will improve communications and make it simpler to deal with emergencies (such as the evacuation of North Bend in face of a forest fire in 1985), there are people who would choose the slower pace and isolation the ferry gave them. The ferry and its operators were the town's security guards and little escaped them!

As 91-year-old resident Harry Lee, who lived in North Bend for 72 years, explained at the opening, "If I want to cross the river I can ride the ferry and talk to the nice girl that works on it and sit in the little hut with the heater and keep warm. Now I'll have to walk across the bridge with the wind blowin' and no one to look after me if I fall off. After 72 years of peace and quiet why would I want a bridge? Do you suppose I could cancel the opening?"

Of course he couldn't; on January 28 Frances Harrington, Cog's widow, cut the ceremonial ribbon.

The west-side road is a reasonable gravel byway. In good weather conditions it can be handled by most drivers with a little backroad experience. A few steep grades reaching 15 degrees need to be negotiated.

Maps

National Topographic Series 1:50,000 92 H/14 Boston Bar; 92 H/13 Skuzzy Mountain; 92 I/4 Lytton or B.C. Lands & Forest Series 1:125,000 92 H/NW Yale; 92 I/SW Lytton.

km 0/mi 0   **km 54.6**/mi 33.9

The starting point for this backroad is the Charles Hotel in Boston Bar. The original Indian village here was called Koia'um. The name Boston Bar, reflecting the fact that Indians called the English "King George men" and Americans "Boston men," referred to a bar on the river where many Americans were panning for gold. The name was later given to the town that formed when the Cariboo Wagon Road came through, followed by the railway. Today it is still a road and rail stop.

In the exciting days of the gold rush, before law and order came to the area, Boston Bar was the centre of hostilities between miners and the Thompson Indians. Angered by the treatment they received from the Americans, the Indians retaliated by murdering small parties of miners, including a party of 15 Frenchmen at Boston Bar.

A skirmish in the canyon country against a party of 25 lasted several days; many of them, including the leader Jack McLennan, lost their lives. Bodies floated down the Fraser and were found bristling with arrows or mutilated in Deadman's Eddy just north of Yale and at Fort Hope. A war party of 150 miners formed at Yale and Boston Bar. In the ensuing battle on August 14, 1858, sometimes referred to as the "battle of Boston Bar," at least two miners and several Indians were killed. Near the end of August, Governor Douglas visited Yale and negotiated a truce with the warring chief, David Spint-lum of Lytton. By November, two advance parties of Royal Engineers had arrived on the mainland and Matthew Baillie Begbie had been sworn in as Chief Justice of the colony.

To begin this side trip, turn west off the Trans-Canada Highway at the Charles Hotel in Boston Bar. Cross the CN railway tracks almost immediately, turn right and go downhill to follow the Fraser.

km 1.0/mi 0.6   **km 53.6**/mi 33.3
  Cog Harrington bridge to North Bend.

km 1.3/mi 0.8   **km 53.3**/mi 33.1
  Lots of spotted knapweed. Those who have travelled backroads over the years may have noticed this plant growing up in many areas. It is a weed that has recently become a serious problem to British Columbia's rangeland.

Knapweed is a native of the Balkans and Asia Minor. Introduced into B.C. in shipments of alfalfa seed from Eurasia before the 1930s, it resembles a small Canada thistle without the leaves. The spiny heads are low in nutritive value, unpalatable to cattle and wildlife, and can cause damage to a grazing animal's mouth and digestive tract. Knapweed is an invader plant with no natural enemies or controls; if it is not halted it could result in the loss of 90 per cent of this province's rangeland by the end of the 1980s.

  Though biological control is the ideal way to prevent the spread of knapweed, this is not a realistic goal until proper controls are developed. In the meantime some action must be taken. As the agency responsible for managing rangeland, the B.C. Forest Serv-

Two shy whitetail fawns find support in the buddy system.

ice has set up the Knapweed Action Committee to direct containment and spraying programs and to co-ordinate interested groups and generally create public awareness of the problem.

Recreationists can help to prevent a takeover of rangeland by knapweed. As it often spreads by being carried on the underparts of vehicles, recreationists should learn to recognize it. They should avoid driving through any infested areas, taking care to check undercarriages and to clear out any plants that have been caught. Sightings of the plant in remote areas should be reported to the District Forest Ranger or the Forest Service Range Management Division. Where just a few plants are found, it is best to pull them up and destroy the seeds. Florists and dried-flower collectors are requested to avoid this weed. Vigilance and precautions now may help to preserve wildlife habitat and the cattle industry.

km 1.4/mi 0.9   **km 53.2**/mi 33.0

Railroad crossing. Railway tracks line both sides of the Fraser from Lytton to the lower Fraser valley. The Canadian Pacific, built in the 1880s to fulfil the promise of Confederation to join east to west with a rail line, follows the canyon on alternate sides to take the easiest route. Here it is on the west side of the river.

Andrew Onderdonk, a young U.S. engineer who gained the contract to construct the 127 miles of rail between Emory's Bar and Savona, was a very resourceful man. He imported laborers from San Francisco and boatloads of Chinese workers; he built a sawmill at Texas Lake, engine and repair shops that could produce railway cars, and a blasting powder factory at Yale that could produce 1200 pounds of explosives a day; he brought in a locomotive that had been used in the building of the Panama Canal and the San Francisco sea wall; and he had a steamer built, called the *Skuzzy,* which plied the perilous canyon rapids to carry supplies to Lytton. Onderdonk's contracts were completed on July 29, 1885; the last spike was driven at Craigellachie on November 7 of the same year.

km 2.2/mi 1.4   **km 52.4**/mi 32.5

Side road. The road to the right leads to the town of North Bend. Situated on an old river terrace, similar to that on which Boston Bar sits, the townsite was once known as "Yankee Flats" or "Yankee Town." These names, with their U.S. connotation, were changed when the CP Railway was constructed; the town became "North Bend" because of its location on the Fraser River.

North Bend, a divisional point on the railway, is an old town with some interesting buildings. The original roundhouse and turntable can still be seen. It was built by Scottish stonemasons brought by Onderdonk from Scotland to construct retaining walls for the railway. The Fraser Canyon Hotel, completed in 1888, was rebuilt in the early 1900s after it burned down. The only store still to be found is in a home. The most fascinating part of a drive through town is to see up close the row of old homes that provides a distinctive feature of North Bend as viewed from the highway across the Fraser. Several of those homes have fallen down in the last few years.

You will find some picnic tables in town. If you detour through North Bend return to the main road and continue north.

Though this is still within the Coastal Forest Zone, the sparse, drier undergrowth indicates that we are approaching the Dry Interior Zone around Lytton. The cedar and fir forest here is interlaced with cottonwood, alder and Douglas maple; roadside shrubs and flowers include Saskatoon berry, Oregon grape, thimbleberry, bracken, fireweed, asters, dogbane and yarrow.

km 3.4/mi 2.1   **km 51.2**/mi 31.8

Gowen Creek culvert passes under the road.

km 4.0/mi 2.5   **km 50.6**/mi 31.4

Bridge over Brunswick Creek. Across the Fraser, Stoyama Creek can be seen draining two small unnamed peaks about 1900 metres in elevation.

Watch and listen for birds in the area. Grosbeaks may be seen in spring and early summer, searching out the seeds that are important to their diet. They are a part of the largest bird family in

Canada, which includes finches, buntings and sparrows. The colors of birds in the *Fringillidae* family vary greatly and include yellows, blues, reds, browns and black; their tail and wing shapes are also variable. However, they all have thick stout bills for crushing seeds.

Another family to be found around here is the *Turdidae* family, represented by bluebirds, solitaires and thrushes; the American robin is probably the most widely recognized member. Again, the appearance of different birds will vary. One thing they have in common, though, is the spotted breasts of their young. The robin breeds almost throughout Canada, except in the very northernmost parts.

km 4.4/mi 2.7   **km 50.2**/mi 31.2

From this point a bridge can be seen crossing Stoyama Creek across the Fraser, carrying a pipeline. A cement abutment near the highway is probably from the old Fraser Canyon highway.

The discovery of gold in the Cariboo began a search for a practical road to the interior through the Fraser Canyon. Contracts were let for various sections, Thomas Spence being given the section between Boston Bar and Lytton, and construction began in 1862. After completion in 1865, the road was used for about 20 years. When the railway came through, the Cariboo Wagon Road fell into disuse and many of the road supports were washed away in the flood of 1894. From then until the end of the First World War, rail was the only means of transport through the canyon.

The Fraser Canyon highway was built between 1924 and 1926, when it was completed as far as Lytton. Like the wagon road, it offered hair-raising travel on cliffs high above the river. The modern road, wider and carved deeper into the rock, is much tamer but still one of the most spectacular routes in British Columbia.

From the vantage point of a good two-lane gravel road on the west bank of the Fraser, it is easy to enjoy the respite from the traffic rushing by on Highway 1 and still appreciate the rugged canyon scenery.

km 5.8/mi 3.6   **km 48.8**/mi 30.3

Side road. The road to the left goes up onto the ridge on the lower reaches of Skuzzy Mountain, whose peak to the southwest reaches 2200 metres. Skuzzy was also the name given to the steamer built by Andrew Onderdonk to carry supplies up the canyon during the construction of the railway. After it was launched on May 4, 1882, Onderdonk had difficulty finding a skipper who would and could navigate the boat up the treacherous Fraser waters. In September,

You may have to look twice to spot grouse in their natural habitat.

the *Skuzzy* was taken from Spuzzum to Boston Bar and then on to Lytton. The little boat must have been a strange sight in the great canyon during the next couple of years as it steamed back and forth. When she was no longer needed her hull was left to float down the Fraser, but her engine was recycled and used in a larger *Skuzzy II* on the Thompson for another 10 years.

km 6.8/mi 4.2   **km 47.8**/mi 29.7

There are several private properties and farms in this area. One pasture was completely taken over by knapweed when we passed by.

km 7.5/mi 4.7   **km 47.1**/mi 29.2

A side road goes down to the right.

km 8.2/mi 5.1   **km 46.2**/mi 28.8

An irrigation flume can be seen up to the left.

km 8.4/mi 5.2   **km 46.2**/mi 28.7

Bridge over Nepopulchin Creek. False box, the attractive shiny shrub along the roadside, is popular in floral arrangements. Unfortunately, this is causing decimation of the profuse stands near areas of population where professional gatherers collect the false box to sell. This bush grows well in rocky areas, and transplants well into gardens.

Grouse, attractive upland game birds, are often glimpsed crossing the road or roosting on stumps or branches.

km 8.8/mi 5.5   **km 45.8**/mi 28.4

After passing an old orchard down to the right, we can see old cabins up to the left. They are constructed of squared logs with dovetailed corners.

km 9.1/mi 5.6   **km 45.5**/mi 28.2

A small creek crosses under the road just before an old mill site. Cinquefoil bloom in large numbers nearby in early summer. The flowers are buttercuplike, usually varying from bright yellow to a very pale yellow or cream, though at least one species is purple. "Cinque" refers to the five leaflets of the flower's palmate leaves. Many of the 200 species also have five petals, five sepals and five bracts. Isolating individual species can be quite difficult; in fact, there is still disagreement amongst botanists about classification of some of the cinquefoils.

km 9.5/mi 5.9   **km 45.2**/mi 28.1

Two bridges cross the split Speyum Creek as it flows down from an unseen peak to the west called The Nipple. Directly across the Fraser from the mouth of Speyum Creek a similar stream drains Stoyama Mountain, which at 2260 metres is slightly lower than The Nipple. The east-side creek is called Ainslie Creek on the top map, but was previously known as Nine-Mile Creek. The highway loops briefly into Nine-Mile Canyon to cross the creek. The Cariboo Wagon Road crossed the creek closer to the Fraser and it was a considerable climb down to traverse Nine-Mile and then up the other side of the creek canyon. There was some respite after the haul, though, at a roadhouse on Jamieson's Flat (Boothroyd to the railway) on the north side of the gorge. Nine miles was the distance from Boston Bar.

If you stop at Speyum Creek for a cool drink of water, beware of the attractive green foliage with inconspicuous greenish flowers. It is stinging nettle, which produces a burning sensation when the tiny hairs come in contact with the skin.

Take time to appreciate all that the senses can offer in the back country. For example, savor the warm summer smell of juniper, difficult to describe but easy to remember.

km 10.1/mi 6.3   **km 44.5**/mi 27.6

A neatly kept, fenced cemetery across the tracks with a tall white cross in the centre is a reminder that the road is passing through an Indian reserve. It is one of many small reserves found on both sides of the Fraser River. Many Interior Salish Indians have inhabited the banks and used the river's resources. Unfortunately, reserves in Canada are usually not large enough for economic survival, with a few exceptions such as the Capilano Reserve in North Vancouver. If they succeed in their land claims, native Indians may yet be able to retain some cultural identity.

km 10.8/mi 6.7   **km 43.8**/mi 27.2

Chamoux. There is still a railway siding at this old railway station. According to CPR records, this is an Indian name meaning "too hot."

km 12.1/mi 7.5   **km 42.5**/mi 26.4

A sign says: "Report forest fires here." The people who live at this place are collectors, judging by the assemblages of pipes, water heaters, tires, trucks, trailers and assorted goods. Just beyond are some cultivated fields. The road passes through forested areas between the ranches and private properties.

km 13.0/mi 8.1   **km 41.6**/mi 25.8

A small creek passes under the road.

km 13.4/mi 8.3   **km 41.2**/mi 25.6

A creek crosses under the road and a powerline overhead. A burned-off area can be seen across the river just ahead.

km 13.9/mi 8.6   **km 40.7**/mi 25.3

Junction. A gate across the road at this point was open when we passed through the area. Keep right to continue along the North Bend to Lytton route.

The left road follows the south bank of the Nahatlatch River about 4 kilometres to a spot where it has been wiped out by a large slide. It used to continue for a couple of kilometres and bridge the Nahatlatch to join up with the roadway into Nahatlatch Lakes. The road passes a landing strip and then winds gently through forested areas and occasional patches of meadow. The grass-lined track gives ample opportunity to observe the shiny-needled grand fir amongst the Douglas fir, red cedar, lodgepole pine, maple and cascara. As well, watch for red elderberry, ceanothus, Devil's club, soopolallie, horsetail, mullein, thistle, buttercup, self-heal, clover and wild strawberry.

The slide across the road, impossible for most vehicles to traverse, did have a few tracks across one area of soft sand. Before turning back, have a good look at the Nahatlatch running clear and green and at the rapids below the slide.

km 14.3/mi 8.9   **km 40.3**/mi 25.0

The road, narrower now than the previous two lanes, goes under the powerline again.

km 15.4/mi 9.6   **km 39.2**/mi 24.3
View of the Fraser. The road heads down to the Nahatlatch.

km 16.2/mi 10.1   **km 38.4**/mi 23.8
Bridge over the Nahatlatch River. In season, the wild rose, daisies, thistle and dogbane make this a pleasant stop. For a good photo, continue a short distance up the road and look back down on the bridge over the fast-flowing waters.

km 16.4/mi 10.2   **km 38.2**/mi 23.7
Junction. This is the "kilometre zero" point for the Nahatlatch backroad, which begins here and goes up to the left; it is described as Route 2 in this book. Many of the vehicles that turn into the Nahatlatch are carrying canoes, kayaks or other watercraft for the lovely mountain lakes and the short streams joining them. Boaters of any kind should not attempt to run the river below the first or lowest lake.

To continue the trip, keep right to the railway tracks and then go up a 16-degree slope to the left. (If this hill seems a little too steep, an alternative is to take the Nahatlatch road and go right when the logging road is reached.)

km 16.8/mi 10.4   **km 37.8**/mi 23.5
Logging road. Keep right; left goes up the Nahatlatch.

km 17.4/mi 10.8   **km 37.2**/mi 23.1
View of the Fraser.

km 19.8/mi 12.3   **km 34.8**/mi 21.6
Side road. The road right goes to Keefers, an old station stop named for George Alexander Keefer, who supervised railway construction between North Bend and Lytton. There is a log dump at Keefers. Also, it was on a bar at Keefers that the dismantled hull of the *Skuzzy* was abandoned. It was somewhat of a tourist attraction until it was washed down the river.

km 21.1/mi 13.1   **km 33.5**/mi 20.8
The side road to the right goes to Keefers cemetery.

km 21.5/mi 13.3   **km 33.1**/mi 20.5
The one-lane rough road, now more or less following the hydro line, climbs a 15-degree slope and continues up a long hill for about a kilometre. On the far side of the Fraser is Mowhokam Creek, with a large slide area visible up the valley. Fireweed, purple asters and thimbleberry line the roadside.

The Trans-Canada Highway can be seen climbing the long hill up the side of Jackass Mountain. In the days of the wagon road, the narrow passage bustled with the mule trains, oxen and horses hauling freight. It was known as the "hill of despair" by early packers. According to a newspaper report the name of the mountain immortalizes a mule that fell through a bridge railing with his load of goods packed for the Cariboo while nearing the top of the long climb in 1863 or 1864. Perhaps the animal just gave up.

(The news item mentioned another incident at the same spot in 1883. A freight wagon loaded with 13,000 pounds of black powder for railway construction blew up, killing driver J.T. Jones and demolishing the wagon. Jones had taught for three years at the provincial boarding school at Cache Creek, which he opened in 1873; then he managed the J. Campbell Hotel there and spent some time in Grand Prairie. He returned in the early 80's to freight on the Cariboo Road.)

Following the printing of this story in 1929, a letter to the editor of *The Province* had another source to suggest: "A party of miners were making their way along the Fraser Canyon before the road was built, following rocky ledges close to the water's edge. One of them remarked that a jackass could not follow such a trail. From this remark the mountain took its name."

The best-known express service of the gold rush was started by Francis Jones Barnard who began his career by carrying a pack and walking the 380 miles from Yale to the Cariboo, and returning in the same manner. The cost was $2 per letter — which makes current postal rates look more reasonable. During the peak of gold production in the Cariboo, Barnard's Express or BX carried out more than $3 million in gold in one year.

A creek in a small canyon goes under the road. It is surrounded by yarrow. The flat whitish flowerhead actually consists of multiple tiny blooms, with notched ray flowers on the outer edge of the cluster and central yellowish disk flowers. The plant grows in dry areas and has a pungent odor when crushed. The name comes from the parish of Yarrow in Scotland. Native people made a tea from the dried leaves of the yarrow and used it topically as a lotion for sore eyes, sprains and bruises.

The waterfall from which Falls Creek takes its name can be seen across the Fraser.

km 27.6/mi 17.1   **km 27.0**/mi 16.8
Moriyama Creek passes under the road; an old orchard is seen to the right.

km 29.4/mi 18.3   **km 25.2**/mi 15.6
Bridge over creek. Ahead is Kwoiek Creek canyon.

km 32.2/mi 20.0   **km 22.4**/mi 13.9
Side road. The road down to the right goes to a log dump. Continue to the left as the road veers away from the Fraser a short distance.

km 32.8/mi 20.4   **km 21.8**/mi 13.5
The trail up Kowiek Creek was at various times an Indian trail, pack trail, forestry trail and mining trail.

Junction. The logging road to the left now follows several miles up the Kwoiek valley to beyond Kwoiek Lake. Keep right to cross the Kwoiek Creek bridge and the road to Lytton. Another side road then branches right to the log dump.

km 33.2/mi 20.6   **km 21.4**/mi 13.3
Side road. A right turn goes down the railway tracks. Just ahead is the Kanaka railway siding. Across the Fraser is Kanaka Bar. The Kanakas were Hawaiian Islanders who were recruited as crewmen for HBC trading ships as early as 1824. Some settled around Fort Langley, giving Kanaka Creek its name; others washed for gold at Kanaka Bar.

km 34.4/mi 21.4   **km 20.2**/mi 12.5
The road climbs at a 15-degree angle and then crosses a flat before another 15-degree climb up a rough steep hill with loose rock.

Listen for the sound of the cicadae, the pulsating buzz in the hot summer air from the male of the species. These large black insects with greenish markings are heard more often than seen, as they inhabit trees and bushes. The resonating organs are located at the base of the abdomen.

km 37.0/mi 23.0   **km 17.6**/mi 10.9
Hyumatko Creek crosses under the road.

km 38.6/mi 24.0   **km 16.0**/mi 9.9
Railway bridges. Two river crossings can be seen below where the CP Railway changes from the west to east bank; to the north, the Canadian National transfers from the east side to the west. The CP bridge, located on what is known as Cantilever Bar, is the original span built by Andrew Onderdonk, his final job in con-

structing the rail line through the canyon. It was the first cantile-
vered bridge to be built in North America and cost about
$300,000. Before this link was completed, freight and passengers
were transported over the Fraser by means of an aerial ferry.

On the Fraser's east side are Siska Lodge and Siska Flats, names
derived from an Indian word. Most sources say that the word
means "uncle"; other indicate that it means "unpredictable,"
perhaps referring to the flow of water in the creek of that name. The
rail stop, which is called Cisco, has the same derivation.

The road at this point is narrow and passes an area of small shale
sides.

km 39.3/mi 24.4   **km 15.3**/mi 9.5

Though slightly marred by powerlines, the view up the Fraser
Canyon is spectacular with its backdrop of Botanie Mountain. This
Indian name refers to the covering of cloud hanging over the
mountain. Botanie Valley was a gathering place of the Interior
Salish tribes for root-digging during May and June in the era when
Indians lived off the land. It is a fine area for backroading and is
described later in this book.

Just ahead on the road is a steep downhill 14-degree grade. The
road deteriorates and is very bumpy with loose rocks. Well into the
Dry Interior Zone now, with ponderosa pine on all sides. This is
the evergreen with the largest needles in the province, usually with
three needles to a cluster. Also known as Western yellow pine, it is
distinguished by orange-red furrowed bark and large rounded
cone. The ponderosa grows in B.C. only in the driest southern
areas such as the Fraser, Okanagan and Similkameen valleys.

km 39.9/mi 24.8   **km 14.7**/mi 9.1

Nahump Creek crosses under the road. On a hot day stop here
for a few moments to freshen up with a cool drink and wash in the
shaded moss-lined creek.

km 40.9/mi 25.4   **km 13.7**/mi 8.5

Pooeyelth Creek, one of several streams draining Klowa Mountain, crosses under the road.

The soopolallie or soapberry bushes growing by the road are
another earmark of the Dry Interior Zone. The dark green small-
leaved bush can be recognized by rustlike marking on the bark and
by silvery hairs and rusty spots on the undersides of the leaves. In
midsummer the almost transparent orange-red berries form in
small clusters. Even a drop of juice from them leaves an unforget-
table, bitter taste in the mouth of the uninitiated. To the Indians,
however, it was a delicacy.

km 41.2/mi 25.6   **km 13.4**/mi 8.3
Side road. The road to the right, signed "Happy Landing," leads down to a ranch.

km 42.8/mi 26.6   **km 11.8**/mi 7.3
Side road to the left; there is a log cabin on the right.

km 43.2/mi 26.8   **km 11.4**/mi 7.1
The road passes over Kamiak Creek. Watch for the delicate mauve-pink-and-white solitary mariposa lilies that grow in the dry soil along the route here.

km 44.2/mi 27.4   **km 10.4**/mi 6.5
There is a ranch here and another about a kilometre farther. Across the Fraser is a sawmill, near Saw Creek. Watch for thistle, wild rose, mullein, Saskatoon berries and wild asparagus.

km 45.7/mi 28.4   **km 8.9**/mi 5.5
Another creek with a fascinating name is passed. This one is called Kwellanak.

km 46.9/mi 29.1   **km 7.7**/mi 4.8
Side road to the left and an orchard below the road. Continue past an abandoned homestead and a couple of newer homes.

km 47.9/mi 29.7   **km 6.7**/mi 42
Bridge over Nikaia Creek. Or, if you prefer, cross by the ford.

km 48.7/mi 30.2   **km 5.9**/mi 3.7
Across the Fraser is the first glimpse of Lytton. The Fraser River, which rises in the Rocky Mountains is 1300 kilometres long and drops 2200 metres before it reaches the sea. The river and its minor tributaries and the McGregor, Nechako, West Road, Quesnel, Chilcotin, Bridge and Thompson drain 231,370 square kilometres, all within British Columbia.

Between Boston Bar and Lillooet, the Fraser lies along what is known as the Fraser River fault zone. Once an older, wider valley 500 to 600 metres above the present river, the granitic, steep-sided gorge was initiated by erosion before the Pleistocene ice age when uplift occurred along the fault line, raising the Coast Mountains. The area was covered with ice during the Pleistocene; this changed the river slightly, leaving traces of meltwater channels at difference levels above it and rounding off some of the mountains.

km 48.9/mi 30.4   **km 5.7**/mi 3.5
Side road. Down to the right is the railway stop of Winch and a railway bridge where the Canadian National crosses the Fraser into

Highway 12 crosses the mouth of the Thompson River where its clear waters mingle with the Fraser.

Lytton. On the far side of the town it crosses the Thompson and continues north on its west side.

km 49.6/mi 30.8   **km 5.0**/mi 3.1

View. The junction of the Fraser and Thompson Rivers can be seen, the clear waters of the Thompson seemingly reluctant to mingle with the muddy flow of the larger waterway. The Highway 12 bridge crosses the Thompson at its mouth. The posts, which can be seen at low water at the mouth of the Thompson, are the remains of an old gold dredge that worked the Fraser above Lytton.

The Indian village at the confluence of these two large rivers was called Camchin, meaning "the great fork." When Simon Fraser stopped there on June 19, 1808, he was greeted by about 1200 natives. In his diary Fraser says: "We had every reason to be thankful for our reception at this place; the Indians shewed us every possible attention and supplied our wants as much as they could. We had salmon, berries, oil and roots in abundance, and our men had six dogs. Our tent was pitched near the camp, and we enjoyed peace and security during our stay."

This was also the site of the Hudson's Bay Company's Fort Dallas; it became a gold-mining camp when placer gold was found

A river-powered reaction ferry links the banks of the Fraser at Lytton.

on the junction bars. In 1858 the town of Lytton was named by Governor Douglas for Sir Edward Bulwer-Lytton, who was Secretary of State for the Colonies.

Today the character of the town has changed. It provides services to local settlers, highway travellers and a growing number of river rafters who use Lytton as the terminus of whitewater runs through the "Jaws of Death" and Pitquah Gorge on the Thompson River.

km 50.3/mi 31.2   **km 4.3**/mi 2.7

The ranch here is on the Papyam Indian Reserve. There is some milkweed by the road, an interesting member of the rubber family.

km 52.3/mi 32.5   **km 2.3**/mi 1.4

Junction. The left road at the T-junction continues up the west side of the Fraser to Lillooet. It is detailed as a backroad in Volume 1 of this series. Take a right turn down to the Fraser.

All through the Fraser canyon the river bars are popular places for anglers. In the fall there is fishing for salmon and rainbow trout, and Dolly Vardens. The creek mouths of all the Fraser tributaries are also good places to check out in the summer months.

km 53.0/mi 32.9   **km 1.6**/mi 1.0

Lytton reaction ferry. An interesting use of the river is made by reaction ferries such as this one, which cross from bank to bank using only the force of the river for power. An operator angles the bow of the pontoon boat into the current by taking a couple of turns around a winch. Then the water pushes the pontoon across the river, while a cable attached to the ferry prevents it from drifting downstream.

The Lytton ferry operates from 5:30 a.m. to 9:30 p.m. seven days a week, except when it is closed for meal breaks from 9:30 to 10:00 a.m. and 5:30 to 6:00 p.m. The service is free, but a $5 toll is charged for emergency trips outside regular hours. As you leave the ferry you reach pavement.

km 53.9/mi 33.5   **km 1.2**/mi 0.7

Junction. Highway 12 to the left goes to Lillooet; keep right for Lytton.

km 54.2/mi 33.7   **km 0.4**/mi 0.2

Side road. The road to the left heads up Botanie Valley.

km 54.6/mi 33.9   **km 0**/mi 0

Bridge over Thompson River. The route ends here just half a kilometre from the town of Lytton, a fine starting point for other explorations.

A little company can sometimes be reassuring . . .

. . . but there's a special thrill in being on your own.

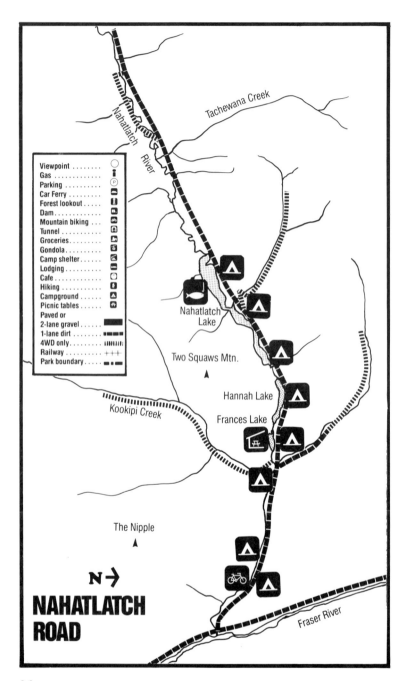

Viewpoint . . . .
Gas . . . .
Parking . . . .
Car Ferry . . . .
Forest lookout . . . . .
Dam . . . .
Mountain biking . . .
Tunnel . . . .
Groceries . . . .
Gondola . . . .
Camp shelter . . . . .
Lodging . . . .
Cafe . . . .
Hiking . . . .
Campground . . . . . .
Picnic tables . . . . . .
Paved or
2-lane gravel . . . . . .
1-lane dirt . . . .
4WD only . . . .
Railway . . . . +++
Park boundary . . . . .

Tachewana Creek

Nahatlatch River

Nahatlatch Lake

Two Squaws Mtn.

Kookipi Creek

Hannah Lake

Frances Lake

The Nipple

N→

NAHATLATCH ROAD

Fraser River

Route Two

Nahatlatch Road

Its fast-running river, emerald lakes and forested hillsides make the Nahatlatch valley an attractive place for recreationists. Reached from the road running north on the west side of the Fraser from North Bend, this area is popular with those who prefer out-of-the-way, quiet places for canoeing, fishing and camping.

The Nahatlatch chain consists of four lakes connected by short streams; it is an easy paddle, but no attempt should be made to run the river below the first or lowest lake as there are grade 5 and 6 rapids on that stretch. Above the lakes is a major log jam. Try fishing for rainbow, cutthroat and Dolly Varden in the lakes and streams, and for winter steelhead, coho and some chinook in the river. Camping is possible beside all the lakes on beaches, which offer several B.C. Forest Service recreation sites and picnic tables. Deer, bear and grouse are likely to be seen.

The Nahatlatch Needle rises above the north side of the highest lake and Two Squaws Mountain above the north side of the area is being logged, but this does not spoil the scenic qualities of the trip. In fact, the logging road provides access into the valley. For most of its length the road is one lane, gravel and fairly good, with wide spots for passing. Be on the lookout for trucks hauling out logs when you use the road on weekdays. There are restrictions on the use of some sections of the route.

The Nahatlatch has become a popular river for kayakers. The upper sections between the three lakes are suitable for open canoes. From Frances Lake to just below Fir Flat recreation site the river's grade 3+ rapids are for intermediates. The canyon below this must be carefully scouted. Check Betty Pratt-Johnson's article in *Whiskey Jack,* July/August 1980, before running. She warns that the rapids have grade 4+ or 5 drops; they can probably be run only in low water in the fall.

Maps

National Topographic Series 1:50,000 92H/13 Skuzzy Mountain; 92 I/4 Lytton or B.C. Lands and Forest Series 1:125,000 92H/NW Yale; 92 I/SW Lytton.

km 0/mi 0

The mileages for this road begin at the junction at the north side of the Nahatlatch River and the west side of the Fraser, 16.4 kilometres north of North Bend. Take a left turn from the West Side road.

km 1.7/mi 1.1

Junction. A D-junction is formed as the road we are following meets up with the logging road into the Nahatlatch. A right turn leads back to the Fraser River and the West Side Road; keep to the left. There is a sign here: "700 Road. B.C. Forest Products Ltd. Boston Bar Division. Use extreme caution. LOGGING TRUCKS HAULING."

km 1.9/mi 1.2

Side road. Goes up to the right.

km 2.1/mi 1.3

Side road. Another road goes up to the right. The Nahatlatch is below on the left; a slide can be seen on the slope above the river.

km 3.5/mi 2.2

The BCFS Apocynum Recreational Site overlooks the Nahatlatch. *Apocynum* is the Latin name for the Dogbane family.

km 4.4/mi 2.7

Shortly after passing a swampy area, you will see another primitive campsite.

km 5.0/mi 3.1

Fir Flat Recreation Site. There is a picnic table and litter barrel at this B.C. Forest Service site.

The most widespread of the firs in B.C. is the Douglas fir, named in 1829 for David Douglas, a Scottish botanist. It grows through most of the southern half of the province and is the largest tree in Canada; the largest specimens grow at the coast. It can be

Serene and unspoiled, the Nahatlatch Valley offers a special welcome to Junction Country explorers.

identified by its flat needles, which are not prickly to touch, and by the downward-hanging cones with three-pronged bracts protruding from under the scales. The wood is strong and widely used in construction and for plywood, flooring and exterior finishing. Interior trees are not as strong but are used for poles, railroad ties and Christmas trees.

km 6.1/mi 3.8

Side road. This road to the left goes only a short distance, ending at an old bridge that crossed the river and connected with a road that once followed up the south side of the Nahatlatch. The south side road no longer goes as far as the bridge, though, as it has been blocked by a slide. Yarrow, wild strawberry and star flower bloomed at the forest edge when we were here in early summer, and a yellow-bellied sapsucker tapped at a milk-run of coniferous trees. A sign points out a trail which runs along the river.

Continue straight on the road parallel to the river, though much of the time it is not in sight. Soon a trapper's cabin is passed.

km 7.3/mi 4.5

The remains of log farm buildings are all that are left of the homestead that once stood in the meadow to the right.

km 8.1/mi 5.0

A creek crosses under the road, one of several that run down from the nameless ridge to the north. Side tracks go off to the right shortly before and after the stream.

The green or greyish growths hanging down from many of the trees are known as old man's beard. This is one of the lichens - primitive plants composed of a fungus and alga. These two have a symbiotic relationship in which each depends on the other for its existence, and together they require only air and moisture. The alga survives by the water-retention properties of the fungus and the fungus by the photosynthesis of the alga.

Old man's beard, which feels like steel wool when dry and like slippery rubber when wet, is high in protein content. It is part of the staple diet of caribou.

Native peoples, early fur traders and explorers sometimes used old man's beard as an emergency food supply in winter, though apparently it was not too palatable. One form of preparation has been suggested to get the best possible taste when it is necessary to eat this lichen. Put a medium-sized stone — not just any old rock, but one that looks good and feels right — and a similar-sized ball of old man's beard into a pot and cover it with water. Boil it up and simmer about 20 minutes until the lichen seems tender. Then throw away the lichen and eat the rock!

km 9.2/mi 5.7

Side road. The road to the left is gated and marked "No trespassing."

km 9.9/mi 6.1

Log Jam Recreation Site. This descriptive (if not especially attractive) name is given to a small site provided by the B.C. Forest Service. Just upriver a tree can be seen in mid-stream at the point on the map where an island is marked.

km 10.5/mi 6.5

Bridge over Log Creek. Just beyond the bridge a road takes off to the right to follow up Log Creek about 10 kilometres, close to its headwaters below glacier-topped Kwoiek Needle. It is an active logging area and a sign indicates that the public may use the road only between 8 p.m. and 5 a.m. from Monday to Saturday, or any time Sundays and holidays. Check with loggers coming out of the area as access is sometimes available a little earlier in the day.

km 10.8/mi 6.6

Continue past the Log Creek Recreation Site. A sign on the main road reminds drivers that logging trucks are hauling. Across the Nahatlatch Kookipi Creek can be seen joining the mainstream.

km 11.0/mi 6.8

Side Road. To the left a road bridges the Nahatlatch and follows Kookipi Creek upstream between Two Squaws Mountain and The Nipple. The sport fishing boundary marked at this point indicates the end of the area closed to angling (downstream as far as the logging bridge). Check the provincial sport fishing regulations for details regarding licensing and restrictions.

km 11.5/mi 7.1

Frances Lake Recreation Site. This site is located on a small lake. The water has a current as it exits the lake toward the river, which is not navigable below this point.

There is an Indian legend about the stalks of mauve-pink fireweed that spring up to cover scars on the land caused by cuts and burns. An Indian woman set fire to the forest around an enemy camp to rescue her lover from torture. He was wounded and as they made their escape they had difficulty keeping ahead of the pursuing foe. But with each footstep of the woman on the burned forest floor, flames sprang up behind them to shield them from their enemies. After the chase was abandoned, fireweed instead of flames rose from the woman's footprints.

km 12.8/mi 7.9

Another small recreation site here is the first of six over the next kilometre. The river below the road joins Hannah and Frances Lakes.

km 13.5/mi 8.4

Hannah Lake Recreation Site.

km 14.1/mi 8.8

Old Hannah Lake ranger station. This solitary cabin set in a beautiful natural location is typical of ranger stations of the past;

This bridge spanning the Nahatlatch River is easier to negotiate than it looks.

it's a pleasant place for reflection on a passing life style. There is fair fishing for rainbow, cutthroat and Dollies in nearby lakes and streams.

km **14.6**/mi 9.1

Firewood and thimbleberry grow below a rockslide along the roadside. Thimbleberry is a shrub with large maple-like leaves. In May and June it is adorned with broad white blossoms, the largest of the flowers borne by any of the local berry bushes. By July and August the blooms are replaced by large round raspberry-like fruit. The thimble name may arise from the hollow in the plucked berry, which is almost thimble-sized. The fruit is edible but more attractive to birds and bears than to people.

km **16.3**/mi 10.1

Some private properties are passed. The cow parsnip found here is a handsome sturdy plant with white flower clusters. Its stems were boiled and eaten by natives and are browsed by mammals such as elk and bear. However, it is not recommended as an edible plant since it is a member of the parsnip family, some of whose species are highly poisonous. Members of the family such as carrot, celery, parsley, dill and parsnip are popular foods, but non of the species should be eaten unless positively identified as non-toxic. Also included in this family is the poison hemlock which Socrates was given when sentenced to death.

An interesting newspaper item relating to this plant family appeared in the Victoria *Colonist* in 1861. Dr. Fiat, a French physician engaged in packing along Fraser River trails, reported: "Leopold, a Greek, ate a piece of the root of a wild turnip, at Davidson's house near Williams Lake, Nov. 22nd and died thirty minutes thereafter. It will be remembered that on the 10th of the same month, a miner named Jourdan died from the same cause. Our informant has analysed some of the root, and finds that it contains a deadly poison known as aqua tofana; the smallest quantity will cause death...The Indians in that vicinity are fond of certain roots; Jourdan and Leopold imagining that they could detect the difference between the poisonous and harmless, undertook to gather them. The result was that they lost their lives. Those proposing to visit that section should bear the fact in mind."

km 16.9/mi 10.5

Nahatlatch Lake Recreation Site. Located at the east end of Nahatlatch Lake is another BCFS campground. The lake has a narrows which almost divides it in two and the river maintains its current the full length.

On our trip into the Nahatlatch we made this site our headquarters and were amazed at the variety of birds in the tall trees. There were also many plants to identify, other wildlife to observe, and a sandy beach as a bonus. Black bears were common.

Sitting quietly on the beach, even a novice can recognize some of the birds. For example, a hummingbird was constantly buzzing the site and blue grouse wandered through the trees with a couple of chicks in tow. Occasionally a robin fluttered by. Higher up in the trees we saw a western tanager, waxwings, pine sisken, Swainson's thrush, evening grosbeaks, bluebirds, tree swallows, a flicker and an unidentified sparrow.

The flora was almost as colorful as the birdlife. Growing beneath the tall cedar, fir and pine were the pinks, mauves, yellow and white of fireweed, spirea, Oregon grape, wild strawberry, twinflower, bunchberry, starflower, pipsissewa, ceanothus, thimbleberry, boxwood and the wild rose. The delicate perfume of the roses added to the garden atmosphere.

The children especially enjoyed the water and aquatic life. More exciting for them than the fish jumping in the lake were minnows darting through the water near shore. They also found the dragonfly nymphs and caddisfly larvae captivating.

To find a caddisfly, look for a tiny collection of twigs and leaves walking on the bottom of a stream, lake or large pond — a caddisfly larva in camouflage. These insects build their own disguise by making themselves shells or cases of minute twigs, grains of sand, small pebbles and leaves held together with a glue-like substance or with silk. As the larva grows it either enlarges its case or builds a larger one. When it is full-grown the larva attaches its case to a rock or other object in the water. Then it pupates, emerging some time later as an adult.

km 18.4/mi 11.4
A creek crosses under the road.

km 18.5/mi 11.5
Salmon Beach Recreation Site. From this site there is a good view of the ridge to the south of the lake, Two Squaws Mountain. Watch for chipmunks scampering along the ground.

km 20.6/mi 12.8
Side road. Another side track goes up to the right. And a little farther up the road is another warning sign that logging trucks are hauling.

km 20.9/mi 13.0
Squakum Recreation Site. Camping is again courtesy of the B.C. Forest Service.

km 21.1/mi 13.1
A large creek flows under the road and another track goes up the large valley to the right, approaching Tachewana Peak. On the north side of the peak are several glacial fields. The Nahatlatch road now climbs up well above the green lake. The banks are steep and there are many boulders.

km 22.6/mi 14.0
The head of Nahatlatch Lake can be seen with a U-shaped valley behind, indicating that a glacier had a part in forming the landscape. To the southwest is Cairn Needle, a needle-shaped peak on a snowcapped mountain. Cairn Needle is midway between Nahatlatch River and Harrison Lake.

km 24.8/mi 15.4
The upper Nahatlatch meanders through the valley amidst large marshy swamps.

km 25.2/mi 15.6

The road goes over another creek. Logging areas can be seen across the valley.

km 27.3/mi 16.9

Side road. Left leads to the river. The roadside is festooned with salsify, oxeye daisies, yarrow, fireweed, lupines and Indian paintbrush.

km 28.5/mi 17.7

A side track goes left.

km 28.8/mi 17.9

Junction. At this V-junction, keep to the right; left leads to the river. The road gradually deteriorates, and eventually is very rough and rocky where a creek has run down it. The end is obviously near!

km 29.8/mi 18.5

Another V-junction. Left leads to the river, a good lunch or fishing spot. There are sandpipers along the beach and gold flecks in the sand. Mines and a mining road can be seen on hills to the east. Be ready for a few mosquitoes.

Keep right at the junction to complete the route. Just ahead is a second junction. Straight ahead is a washed-out bridge. A ford below is suitable for 4x4s but we chose the easier way and continued to the right. Before going on through we stopped for a few minutes at the large wild strawberry patch. Early July was a perfect time to harvest the small but sweet red berries. The runners by which the plant spreads were very obvious between each of the plants; they seem to explain the name, as they help to "strew" the fruit about the ground.

km 30.6/mi 19.0

The road has become very narrow and has deteriorated to the point where it seemed pointless to continue. Hikers or 4x4s may wish to continue further. There is still the return trip to enjoy, back through the mountain valley, past quiet lakes and a fast running river to its mouth at the Fraser River.

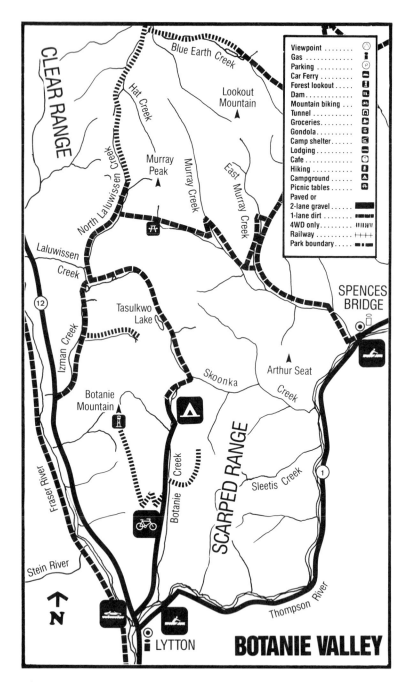

BOTANIE VALLEY

Route Three

Botanie Valley

"Botanie Valley situated in the mountains, some ten miles from Spences Bridge and about fifteen miles from Lytton, has been of time immemorial a gathering place for the upper divisions of the tribe, chiefly for root-digging during the months of May and June. Sometimes over a thousand Indians representing all of the divisions of the tribe would gather there." This description, written by James Teit in a report on the Thompson Indians published in 1900, indicates the importance to the native people of this beautiful valley with its abundance of flora and fauna.

As in earlier days, it remains a mecca for those who enjoy wild flowers; there is a great diversity of plant life along the streams and lakes, in grassy fields, on the forest floor and in the alpine meadows. Though there is only one BCFS recreation site within the valley, you will find many quiet places to stop for a picnic or to wander around and enjoy the flowers. Also, Botanie Mountain offers spectacular views of the Fraser and Thompson Valleys and its upper slopes are ideal for walking or hiking.

Four roads lead into Botanie Valley; at least one of them is always passable. For this book we have chosen to enter the valley from the road leading north from Lytton and to describe each of the other three routes in turn as possible exits. Return mileages are given from the beginning of the route at Lytton to the exit west to Highway 12 via Izman Creek; then we describe the road up North

Alpine meadows light up the Botanie Valley.

Laluwissin Creek to the Hat Creek divide, with one-way mileages; finally, the east exit out of Murray Creek to Spences Bridge is detailed with return mileages from Lytton to Highway 1 at Spences Bridge.

There are several side roads, one to the alpine meadows on Botanie Mountain and another through a logging area around Izman Creek. The road into the valley from Lytton is partially paved and then gravel and should not be a problem for any vehicle. The exit routes become quite rough in spots but are passable in dry weather. In the occasional rains that hit the area the roads become very slick and (as proved by our experience on the North Laluwissin) like gumbo or "loon-dung," as the locals call it. So try and choose a dry time to visit the valley and go prepared for the unexpected.

The route would be a pleasant one for mountain biking. It does not have the steep grades associated with other routes and offers the advantage of several loops back to Lytton.

Maps

National Topographic Series 1:50,000 92 I/4 Lytton; 92 I/ 5 Stein River; 92 I/6 W Spences Bridge; 92 I/12 E Lillooet or B.C. Lands and Forest Series 1:25,000 92 I/SW Lytton; 92 I/NW Ashcroft.

km 0/mi 0   **km 42.6**/mi 26.4

The bridge over the Thompson River at Lytton marks the starting point for the route through Botanie Valley.

When Simon Fraser made his famous descent of the Fraser in 1808 he recorded in his diary many sightings of Indian encampments along the river and many encounters with different groups of natives, usually of a friendly and helpful nature. Often the Indians would accompany his party along the river or trail, as well as offering food and directions. It was at Lytton that Fraser met up with a large group of the "Hacamaugh (Thompson Indian) nation" that he estimated at about 1200. He shook hands with all of them and was welcomed with a long speech and feasting. Then the Indians sang and danced all night.

The Thompson Indians are part of the Interior Salish of the Fraser, who are found from approximately the Quesnel Lakes south into Washington and Idaho, excepting the Kootenay region. The four major tribes in British Columbia within this culture group are the Thompsons, Okanagans, Lillooets and Shuswaps. Each occupied an area of the interior plateau and formed a distinct group, though they have many characteristics in common.

The physiographic relief of the plateau country provided a wide altitudinal variety in resources that were used by the Interior Salish people. They were somewhat nomadic, but did establish fairly permanent winter villages. Food gathering was time-consuming, so the high level of art found in coastal people was not evident among the Interior Salish.

km 0.5/mi 0.3   **km 42.1**/mi 26.1

Junction. The highway ahead goes to Lillooet. For the Botanie route, turn right on a paved road that quickly becomes gravel, following along the Thompson for a short distance and gradually climbing. It was Fraser who named this river "Thompson's river" in recognition of Kootenae House being built by David Thompson in 1807. Fraser thought the fort was located on the upper reaches of the Thompson; in fact, it was on the Columbia. David Thompson never saw the river that bears his name. Later the larger river at this confluence was named by Thompson in honor of Simon Fraser.

Note the deposits along the side of the road where the Thompson has cut through an older river bed.

km 3.1/mi 1.9   **km 39.5**/mi 24.5

Giant escarpment. Where the road leaves the Thompson and begins to follow up Botanie Creek, there is a granitic ridge sometimes called "The Crag." It is cut off vertically on the west by a fault scarp while the eastern side has a fairly regular gentle slope.

The escarpment is likely a result of a fault in this area of contact between the Coast Range batholith and Paleozoic shitose rock.

km 5.3/mi 3.3   **km 37.3**/mi 23.2

The route leads past small farms, ranches and homesteads. Sometimes farm products are offered for sale, such as home-grown eggs. This is ponderosa pine, sagebrush and balsam root country, typical of the Dry Interior Zone east of the mountains that have drained most of the moisture from the clouds. The annual rainfall in this zone averages about 38 centimetres with hot summers and relatively mild winters.

Ponderosa pine, also known as bull pine, jack pine, yellow pine and B.C. pine, is officially *Pinus ponderosa.* Identifiable by its long green needles in bunches of three and its orange ridged bark, the ponderosa is closely associated with bunchgrass and cattle country. Although it is a useful wood for making boxes, it offers its greatest appeal when it stands in its natural parklike setting surrounded by grass.

Sage, sagebrush or *Artemesia tridentata* usually indicates overuse of grasslands. When settlers came to the plateau area they released stock onto ranges and eventually overgrazed it to such an extent that the bunchgrass could not keep the sage from taking over. The identification of sage is made easy by remembering the Latin word *tridentata* or "three teeth." Each leaf of the sage has three small teeth. The pungent smell of sage can be enjoyed by a walk through the brush or from a sprig in your vehicle.

The showy yellow sunflowers with large greyish-green arrowhead shaped leaves are *Balsamorhiza sagittata,* more commonly called balsam root. Often slopes are almost covered with these sunshiny plants when their blooms are at a peak, usually in May. For natives they were an important summer food resource. The numerous oily seeds were mixed with deer grease and boiled in bark baskets by putting hot stones into the mixture. The large roots, gathered by the Indian women using digging sticks, were roasted in pit-ovens and then ground into flour. The young shoots may have been eaten as well.

km 6.9/mi 4.3   **km 35.7**/mi 22.2

Side road. To the right a road cuts back through some private properties on the lowest reaches of the mountains between Botanie and the Thompson River, called the Scarped Range.

km 7.4/mi 4.6   **km 35.7**/mi 21.9

Side road. The track to the left goes through private property and joins up with the Botanie Mountain access road.

Botanie Mountain provides a good view of Lytton (seen here, top right) where the Thompson and Fraser Rivers meet.

The wild rose seen by the road is a flower that has inspired poets and songwriters. There are several different species of wild rose in B.C. varying from white to deep rose, all with a delicate and memorable fragrance. The fruit after the bloom is called a "hip" and is a good source of Vitamin C. It can be dried and used as tea or boiled with a little sweetening to make syrup or jam. It is also delicious when cooked up half-and-half with apples, put through a sieve and made into jelly.

km 9.2/mi 5.7   **km 33.4**/mi 20.7

Side road. Botanie Mountain Lookout Road goes off to the left. Driving or climbing up this road may be the highlight of an excursion to the Botanie area for those who enjoy identifying or photographing wild flowers. As well, there are superb aerial views of the surrounding landscape to reward those who make the ascent. The road is steep for much of its length and not all vehicles will make it to the top. My van went 11.1 kilometres up from this junction, well into alpine territory and within a few hundred yards of the old fire lookout tower.

The Botanie lookout road winds about 1.9 kilometres southward to a fork, then after a right turn climbs steeply with sharp hairpin turns. It passes an old burn area and many colorful roadside flowers, reaching the first superb view of Lytton at 4.5 kilometres. There are signs along the way marking locations like Moose Flats, Devil's Leap, and Tony's Bear Camp.

It would not be possible to list all the wild flowers of the mountain, but many were recognizable; for example, we saw tiger lily, yarrow, paintbrush (masses of it in some spots), lupine, wild rose, columbine, balsam root, thimbleberry, ceanothus, soopolallie, wild strawberry and spreading phlox. The mountain ladyslipper, though, was the rarest flower that we discovered there and were able to photograph. We also found a sparrow hawk, robins . . . and quite enough mosquitos. At 11.1 kilometres a steep, loose-gravel slope prevented us from continuing; and after two or tree tries, we backed up a short distance before turning around.

The old lookout is at an elevation of 6548 feet and considerably south of the main peak of Botanie Mountain. Originally "Bootahnie," this mountain was named by the Indians for the cloud that often hung over it. The creek, lake and an Indian reserve have all taken their name from the mountain, with the reserve retaining the earlier spelling.

Back at the 9.2-kilometre junction on the main road, continue north for Botanie Lake.

km 10.0/mi 6.2   **km 32.6**/mi 20.2
Side road. The road to the right crosses Botanie Creek and then climbs across the mountainside for about 4 kilometres. The rock bluffs to the east are still a part of the Scarped Range.

km 11.2/mi 7.0   **km 31.4**/mi 19.4
After a couple of hesitant patches the pavement ends.

km 11.8/mi 7.3   **km 30.8**/mi 19.1
Baldhill Creek Crossing.

km 15.8/mi 9.9   **km 26.8**/mi 16.6
Bridge over Botanie Creek. The road crosses to the east side of the creek here and then back to the west side in about one kilometre.

km 17.1/mi 10.6   **km 25.5**/mi 15.8
Huckleberry Creek Crossing.

km 17.4/mi 10.8   **km 25.2**/mi 15.6
Botanie Lake, dammed at its south end, stands at the southern end of the Bootahnie Indian Reserve. In the lake area are many of the flowers mentioned and several other lesser-known plants such as the dainty false forget-me-nots, field chickweed, purple larkspur, and trumpet-shaped penstemon. Tiger lilies scattered about the grass have an onion-like bulb that can be eaten if cooked well to remove the starchy taste. Natives cooked them by steaming in underground pits, saving the smallest roots to replant for the following year's crop.

There's lots of open sky and open space along the Botanie Road.

An Indian myth about the Botanie Valley is related by James Teit. He says that the abundance of fleshy roots and underground stems "is accounted for by the Thompson River tribes as due to a powerful woman who lived at Lytton. She was taken away by a great chief, some say the Sun. She wanted to leave provisions for her people so she dropped edible roots at Botanie, saying that 'roots will grow in abundance in this place; and all my children shall repair here to dig them.'"

Birds are often found in the lake area — sandpipers and killdeer plovers in the sand and gravel, robins and flickers in the trees, and nighthawks ghosting through the air at dusk. There is a view of Botanie Mountain lookout to the south.

km 17.8/mi 11.0   **km 24.8**/mi 15.4
Botanie Lake Recreation Site is a small semi-open site with good access for cars. In dry weather it would also be suitable for motorhomes. There is good fishing for rainbows on the fly or by trolling.

km 17.9/mi 11.1   **km 24.7**/mi 15.3
A cattle guard and gate. Leave gates as you find them. This is the beginning of the Bootahnie Indian Reserve.

km 18.1/mi 10.7   **km 24.5**/mi 15.7
Botanie Lake Dam on the right. The road deteriorates here to one lane of rough gravel.

53

km 19.5/mi 12.1   **km 23.1**/mi 14.3

Having left Botanie Creek behind at Botanie Lake, the road now follows along Skoonka Creek for a few kilometres. Our route is upstream as Skoonka Creek flows east and drains into the Thompson River canyon.

km 20.0/mi 12.5   **km 22.6**/mi 14.0

Road to the right. Stay left. This road leads up Skoonka Creek.

km 20.6/mi 12.8   **km 22.0**/mi 13.7

Soon after crossing Skoonka Creek we find Inchawka Creek flowing in from the right.

km 21.8/mi 14.0   **km 20.2**/mi 12.3

There has been some recent logging in this area and several short-haul roads branch off the main route. They can make interesting exploring and often loop back to the main route. Stay straight to stick with the detailed mileages.

km 23.7/mi 14.7   **km 18.9**/mi 11.7

Pasulko Lake. Seen through the trees to the left, the lake drains into the Fraser River to the east via Laluwissin Creek. A side road goes left here. Stay right.

In addition to providing the Interior Salish people with a source of food in the form of roots and berries, this valley also had many of the trees used in their manufacture of vessels for the gathering, cooking and storing of those foods. Birch bark, spruce root, cedar root, cherry bark and willow were the materials most commonly used for birch-bark baskets or pails.

Cedar roots went into the coiled baskets at which the Lower Thompson and Lillooet groups excelled. The roots were usually dug in early summer when the ground was unfrozen and the sap was running, making them more pliable and easier to pierce. The digging and prying sticks used to uncover and lift the roots were made of antlers from deer or elk, or from lengths of hardwood slightly bent with a pointed tip. The tip was sometimes burned to toughen it, and a perforated handle of wood or bone could be used on either end of the shaft.

km 24.6/mi 15.2   **km 18.0**/mi 11.3

The Pasulko Lake Indian Cultural Camp is on the left. We now enter Nananahout Indian Reserve.

km 25.1/mi 15.6   **km 17.5**/mi 10.9

In the swampy area between Pasulko Lake and a smaller marshy lake just ahead, the grass becomes bright with snapdragon-shaped monkey flowers in early summer. Seen up close, the yellow blooms have brown or purple speckles on the lower lip. A native plant of North America, the monkey flower has been introduced in Europe and is now wide-spread there.

km 25.6/mi 15.9 **km 17.0**/mi 10.6
Marshy lake. On the Department of Surveys and Mapping sheet 92I/5, 1:50,000, 1975, the road ends here. However, as we can see, it does continue to complete the route out of the valley.

km 26.7/mi 16.6 **km 15.9**/mi 9.9
End of Bootahnie Indian Reserve. Beyond here, active logging in 1985 often made the road a little confusing and muddy.

km 27.7/mi 17.2 **km 14.9**/mi 9.2
A small stream to be forded, the first of three over the next 4 kilometres. We soon pass through a meadow with an old cabin.

km 30.5/mi 18.9 **km 12.1**/mi 7.5
Turnip Lake.

km 32.0/mi 19.9 **km 10.6**/mi 6.7
Watch for a beaver lodge. The fur trade, which could accurately be called the beaver trade, was responsible for the exploration and early development of Western North America. For centuries the pelt of the beaver dominated the fur trade, for the animal was born with a fatal flaw: the hairs on its rich underfur, called "muffoon," were microscopically barbed. The barbs meant beaver fur felted up better than any other, and in a time when felt hats were in vogue it gave them a value that built huge monopolies such as the Hudson's Bay Company and created a unique breed of men — the mountain men. In their quest for beaver streams they opened the west and were followed by settlers. The trade died when fashion switched to silk hats, and only just in time; beaver were becoming scarce everywhere, and virtually extinct in many areas. The shift in fashion, however, made it possible for the beaver to make a comeback.

km 32.2/mi 20.0 **km 10.4**/mi 6.5
The old junction used to be at this point but work on the dam and reorientation of the roads has moved it on to km 34.7.

km 33.5/mi 20.8 **km 9.1**/mi 5.7
Junction. To the right is the Coldwater-Hat Creek B.C. Forest Service Fire Access Road; to the left is the road that leads via Izman Creek to Highway 12. From this junction three alternate routes out of the Botanie valley area will be detailed. The first to be covered is the most westerly route, Izman Creek Road, which ends

at Highway 12. Those who wish to take the North Laluwissin or Murray Creek exits should read ahead.

Izman Creek Road
To continue west, keep to the left. Open grassy flats, overlooking a small lake with an earthen dam at one end, make a pleasant place to stop and explore, or picnic and camp. Many prickle-protected thistles and wild roses are around, and golden-eyes are often seen on the lake. The remains of a cabin are nearby. To complete the rural scene, cows are usually grazing in the meadow.

km 32.4/mi 20.1   **km 10.2**/mi 6.3
After crossing a small tributary of Laluwissin Creek, the road curves around the lake and proceeds southward.

km 32.9/mi 20.4   **km 9.7**/mi 6.0
Side road. Continue straight where a side track goes off to the left.

km 34.9/mi 21.7   **km 7.7**/mi 4.8
Cattle gate. Though not too many wet days occur in this dry interior zone, when there is a little rain the road becomes slick very quickly. We pass through several open areas with young trees. Wild flowers noted in driving by were stonecrop, oxeye daisies and arnica.

km 36.1/mi 22.4   **km 6.5**/mi 4.0
Side road. To the left a side road goes up onto the ridge. Keep straight on the main road, descending into the valley by parallelling Izman Creek. This area has been logged. Two forms of lichen are seen on trees nearby — letharia and old man's beard.

km 36.8/mi 22.8   **km 5.8**/mi 3.6
Side road. A logging road takes off to the right and winds 9 kilometres around the hill that stands between Izman Creek and the Fraser River. By following the logging road and keeping to the left, we reach a point with a view overlooking the Fraser. In the grass under the trees are many balsam root plants and wild onion.

The nodding onion, *Allium Cernuum,* is the most common of the edible onions found in B.C. It is easily recognized by its bent or "nodding" flowerhead of a dozen or so mauve-pink flowerlets. It blooms from mid-May to mid-July. The leaves are grass-like and rise from a bud similar to that of a common green onion.

Early explorers and Indians used the wild onion to add flavor to their diet. Alexander Mackenzie mentions feasting on these small spring onions on his way to the Arctic Ocean. Simon Fraser writes that his party "gathered some wild onions for sauce," and on two other occasions tells of being given wild onions by the Thompson Indians. According to one source, onions were sometimes steamed by the Thompson Indians in pits in the ground, and were flavored with the leaves and flowers of the "hummingbird plant." On a trip through the back country, the bulbous roots of the nodding onion make a perfect addition to a salad, soup or stew.

km 37.7/mi 23.4   **km 4.9**/mi 3.0
After an open area in the trees a small creek crosses the road. Then the descent to the highway continues. Complementing the pine and fir forest covering the hillside is a wide selection of plants: ceanothus, juniper, brown-eyed susans, thin goldenrod, wild rose, mariposa lily, dogbane, thistle, nodding onion, ocean spray, fire-weed, purple aster, yarrow salsify, soopolallie and wild raspberry.

km 41.5/mi 25.8   **km 1.1**/mi 0.7
Cattle gate. The final steep descent is on a zig-zagging one-lane gravel road with pullouts. Again, it is slippery when wet. Use a low gear and watch your brakes.

km 42.6/mi 26.4   **km 0**/mi 0
Highway 12. The backroad meets the highway 18.7 kilometres north of the bridge over the Thompson River at Lytton. For those who may wish to enter Botanie Valley from this point, the Izman road is tricky to spot. Coming north from Lytton the forest access road goes right just before a hairpin turn. This is the end of the Izman Creek section. The options here are to head north to Lillooet or south to Lytton.

Coldwater-Hat Creek Road

km 32.2/mi 20.0
Junction. Back at the junction, 32.2 kilometres from Lytton, there are two alternate exits besides Izman Creek out of Botanie Valley. Go north on the Coldwater-Hat Creek Forest Road for both options. A junction 6.3 kilometres up this road is where the Murray Creek road leaves the North Laluwissin route.

The road passes through trees edging a meadow enclosed by an old snake fence. A snake fence is expensive to build without one's own trees for raw materials. It is a strong fence, using some 2500 logs per mile and often lasting up to 40 years.

km 33.2/mi 20.6
Old millsite. An old road junction seen down to the left probably followed Laluwissin Creek; though marked on some maps, it does not appear to be in use now.

57

The skies over Botanie Valley continue to look good.

km 34.2/mi 21.2

Culvert over Laluwissin Creek. From here the graded gravel road follows the North Laluwissin, winding up and down through pine-fir forests and open meadows.

km 35.5/mi 22.0

Cattle guard. There has been recent logging in this area.

km 36.2/mi 22.5

Side road. After a culvert under the road is crossed, a side road which has been scarified goes off to the left. The surrounding land has been selectively logged. Below the trembling aspen are stonecrop, arnica, sticky geranium, penstemon, vetches, yarrow, soopolallie and kinnikinnick. The leaves of the kinnikinnick or bearberry were often used by the natives or explorers as a tobacco substitute or extender. Its berries were eaten or crushed and used as a lotion.

km 37.7/mi 23.4

A logging road to the right or east.

km 38.5/mi 23.9

Junction. The road to the right, Murray Creek Road, follows Murray Creek to its mouth near Spences Bridge. It is described following **km 45.1** of this route.

Continue left along the North Laluwissin to get through to Blue Earth Creek. Although shown on maps as continuing through to Upper Hat Creek, the route has been closed by a locked gate. The Blue Earth Road is the only exit.

The road continues through parklike forested areas with the bright colors of lupine, wild rose, paintbrush, penstemon and vetches dotting the grass.

km 39.3/mi 24.4
After another creek is crossed, the road continues gradually uphill towards the pass.

km 40.5/mi 25.1
The road descends to cross another creek and then begins climbing again. The large numbers of lupine form a blue mosaic with the green grass.

km 42.1/mi 26.1
Gate. The road is rockier and the North Laluwissin, now just a small brook, can be seen on the left.

km 42.9/mi 26.6
The road crosses another creek and continues to climb gradually up, passing a willow meadow. Now and then paintbrush, columbine or wood betony are glimpsed under the trees.

km 43.8/mi 27.2
The road deteriorates, becoming more of a track and made worse by a creek running over it. The scenery continues to be attractive — many tiny flowers in the willow meadow along the dwindling creek, with a small cabin or line shack.

km 45.1/mi 28.0
This becomes the final mileage on this road as the rain turns the road to gumbo, too slippery to continue the few remaining metres to the top of the pass and almost too muddy to back up and turn around. In fact, we spent a couple of hours winching our van back onto the road after it kept slipping sideways while we attempted to back up. On a more recent trip the rain (which I always seem to hit in this near-desert area) halted us a kilometre earlier.

The road does continue over a pass and down Hat Creek. However, the road beyond the pass has several stream fords, some of which are quite difficult and suitable only for 4x4s or pickups. We tried the road in the opposite direction, from Blue Earth, and were again stopped by steep grades and mud. The Blue Earth-Hat Creek junction and the locked gate are approximately 9 km away. See the Blue Earth Road for more details.

Murray Creek Road

km 38.5/mi 23.9   **km 27.5**/mi 17.1

Now the final exit from Botanie Valley is considered, with return mileages given from Spences Bridge. At the **km 38.5** junction turn east onto the Murray Creek Road. Along the one-lane road are many of the bushes and flowers already mentioned that grow in the shelter of the fir-pine forest.

The division of labor into men's and women's activities, as practised by the Interior Salish, determined that berries and roots were collected by the women. Usually a small basket was carried around the neck for berry picking; when full it was emptied into larger birch-bark baskets. For root digging the small basket could be carried on the back.

Apparently when soopolallie berries were picked the berries were shaken off the branch into a basket held under it. The berries could be eaten fresh or dried by simmering out some of the juice and drying in the sun; they could be soaked in hot water before they were used. Or the berries could be made into "skahooshum" or "Indian ice-cream," considered a special treat by the children. This confection is made by taking a couple of tablespoons of soopolallie and whipping them into a froth. It can be sweetened with wild strawberries, raspberries or sugar, and is beaten until it has a meringue-like consistency. Even modern children accustomed to an overabundance of sweets can quickly acquire a taste for this tart dessert.

km 39.4/mi 24.5   **km 26.6**/mi 16.5

Creek under road.

km 40.9/mi 25.4   **km 25.1**/mi 15.6

A marshy area is seen to the right and a small creek crosses the road. The road is descending now, following the upper reaches of Murray Creek.

km 43.4/mi 27.0   **km 22.6**/mi 14.0

Junction. A logging road goes left and we then ford over the west fork of Murray Creek. The BCFS has a small recreation site here. A couple of new flowers are seen — twinflower and stinging nettle. Black bear live in the area, judging by the droppings.

km 46.4/mi 28.9   **km 19.4**/mi 12.0

The road has gradually changed character, having been recently graded. It descends steeply.

km 47.7/mi 29.6   **km 18.3**/mi 11.4

Cattle gate. The road crosses over Murray Creek.

Black bears are best avoided. They don't want to meet you, either.

km 48.0/mi 30.0   **km 18.0**/mi 11.2
Junction with an old road.

km 48.7/mi 30.2   **km 17.3**/mi 10.7
A rough track heads up the east side of Murray Creek.

km 49.2/mi 30.5   **km 16.8**/mi 10.4
A side road coming in from the right leads to an active logging area. The main road is one lane and good gravel with pull-offs, almost two lanes in spots. There are ceanothus (a popular browsing plant of deer), flat-topped spirea and pineapple weed in the open forest areas.

km 52.0/mi 32.3   **km 14.0**/mi 8,7
A side road to the left is now ditched. Keep straight.

km 52.8/mi 32.8   **km 13.2**/mi 8.2
Junction. The left arm of the V goes up East Murray Creek (sometimes Hume Creek) through the Venables Valley and is listed as a separate route. Continue right for Spences Bridge. Keep right; about 0.1 kilometres further, another track goes off to the left.

km 53.5/mi 33.2   **km 12.5**/mi 7.8

Junction. A left turn follows up the east side of a small creek and then joins up with the Venables Valley road.

km 54.4/mi 33.8   **km 11.6**/mi 7.2

Old corral.

km 55.3/mi 34.3   **km 10.7**/mi 6.6

Side road. Off to the right is a logging road. Continue straight on the road ahead which is working gradually downhill, passing through cottonwoods, and winding up and down high above the creek.

km 58.2/mi 36.1   **km 7.8**/mi 4.8

Cattleguard. The road seems to have been squeezed between a rock wall and the creek. There are still flowers and berries along the roadside, including mullein, dogbane, raspberries and Saskatoons.

km 59.0/mi 36.6   **km 7.0**/mi 4.3

Bridge over Murray Creek. This is the first of three crossings back and forth across the creek over the next 0.5 kilometres. The creek is named for John Murray who in 1885 was described by Newton Chittenden as "an old time resident." He had a ranch at the mouth of the creek where he grew grain, vegetables, apples, cherries, plums and berries.

km 59.9/mi 36.9   **km 6.5**/mi 4.0

Slide area. The loose gravel hanging above the road may sometimes be a problem here. As the road continues to wind along by the creek, watch for Bighorn sheep across the gully. A small band of Rocky Mountain Bighorn sheep were brought into the Spences Bridge area in 1927 and are sometimes seen on these hills. Bighorn sheep are thought to have arrived in North America after crossing the Bering Straits by a land bridge 25,000 to 40,000 years ago. Vast ice fields still covered most of North America, ice fields that would raise the level of the oceans as they melted to flood out the land bridge. In the very dry ground are a couple of interesting flowers scattered through the sage and rabbit bush. These are mariposa lilies and milkweed.

Like many of the desert flowers, the mariposa lily is very inconspicuous; its single pale blooms may go unnoticed in the stark environment until they are almost walked upon. The flowers have a delicate beauty befitting the name "mariposa": Spanish for "butterfly." The coloring of the tuliplike bloom is usually pale mauve or pink, but sometimes varies to purple or white. The three large petals have green markings towards the centre of the flower. Usually the foliate consists of one thin leaf rising from the base of the stem. The bulblike root was eaten by the Indians.

A much sturdier-looking plant seen right at the roadside is the milkweed. It has large leathery leaves and stands from 0.5 to 1.5 metres high. The broad composite rose-tinged bloom is made up of many small flowers, each with a complicated structure to ensure cross-pollination by the bees and butterflies attracted to the sweet nectar. The name of this plant arises from its unusual property of exuding a white milk-like sticky fluid from a leaf or stem if pricked or torn. This protects the flowers from the sharp-clawed ants and beetles that become trapped in the tacky exudate. The seed pods, which appear in the fall, are large and contain thousands of silken hairs, each attached to a seed. Dispersed by the wind, they parachute to new locations.

A colorful orange-red beetle with black spots that we found on a milkweed plant near here turned out to be an interesting insect. Checking it out, we found it was a four-eyed milkweed beetle. This is one of several insects that feed on the milkweed successfully. The gaudy color is thought to be a protection from birds by warning that they are milkweed eaters and therefore taste bitter.

km 62.8

Side road. To the left, a side road leads to an old homestead. A short walk provides a view of Murray Creek canyon.

km 63.0/mi 39.1   **km 3.0**/mi 1.9

A view of the falls near the mouth of Murray Creek can be had by walking a short distance along a side track to the left. From here the road descends quickly.

The road winds across an old slide area. In 1885 Chittenden described it as "the great mud slide, or moving mountain, which a railroad engineer said was sliding toward the river at the rate of eight feet a year. How to build a railway over this changing base, is a problem the engineers are trying to solve."

They did solve the problem but 20 years later a great landslide occurred, described by a stop-of-interest sign on the Trans-Canada Highway:

"Suddenly on the afternoon of August 13, 1905, the lower side of the mountain slid away. Rumbling across the valley in seconds, the slide buried alive five Indians and dammed the Thompson River for over four hours. The trapped waters swept over the nearby Indian village drowning 13 persons."

CPR engineer H.J. Cambie put the cause down to excess irrigation that led the soil to lose adhesion.

A one-lane road follows Murray Creek to its mouth near Spences Bridge.

km 64.1/mi 39.8   **km 1.9**/mi 1.2

Gate and railway crossing. The cascading waterfall on Murray Creek can be seen up to the left. On a hot Spences Bridge summer day, a walk up to the fall and under its spray is an ideal way to cool down. At one time a hermit lived below the waterfall in a small shack, but he had to find a more remote existence when too many people came to see the cascade for themselves. Now it is a popular spot with river rafters as well as backroaders and adventurous tourists.

km 64.8/mi 40.2   **km 1.2**/mi 0.7

The Trans-Canada Highway bridge crosses overhead. Fishermen on the shore and along the bars of the Thompson River are likely angling for trout or salmon: Kamloops trout through the summer, steelhead trout in the winter months, and salmon (coho and spring) in the fall. Check the Sport Fishing Regulations put out by the Fish and Wildlife Branch annually for details on closures and regulations.

km 65.3/mi 40.5   **km 0.7**/mi 0.4

Railway crossing. The road continues through the CNR yards of Spences Bridge. Once an Indian gathering place, Spences Bridge became known as Cook's Ferry when between 1862 and 1865 the Thompson River was crossed by a cable ferry run by Mortimer Cook. Cook arrived with only a mule and his own determination. In a few years he had made a small fortune and retired to California where he became a mayor and banker. In the financial crash of 1877 he lost all his funds to his creditors.

After the completion of the Cariboo Wagon Road, a bridge was built by Thomas Spence for which a toll was charged. The settlement became "Spence's Bridge."

km 65.6/mi 40.7   **km 0.4**/mi 0.2

Junction. Take a left towards the highway.

km 66.0/mi 41.0   **km 0**/mi

Highway 1 at Spences Bridge. This is the end of the description of the roads passing through the Botanie Valley, one of the most attractive areas of the Interior Plateau.

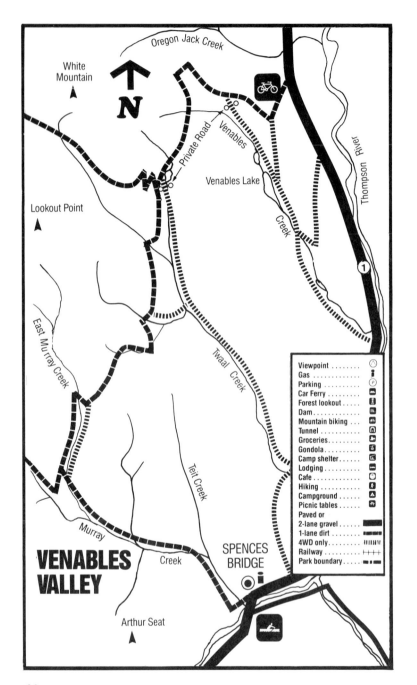

Oregon Jack Creek

White
Mountain

N

Private Road — Venables

Venables Lake

Lookout Point

Creek

Thompson River

1

East Murray Creek

Twaal Creek

Teit Creek

Viewpoint	⊘
Gas	⛽
Parking	Ⓟ
Car Ferry	⛴
Forest lookout	🔭
Dam	🌊
Mountain biking ...	🚲
Tunnel	🚇
Groceries.........	🛒
Gondola..........	🚡
Camp shelter......	⛺
Lodging	🏠
Cafe	☕
Hiking	🥾
Campground	🏕
Picnic tables	🍴
Paved or 2-lane gravel	▬▬▬
1-lane dirt	▰▰▰
4WD only.........	⸽⸽⸽⸽
Railway	+++
Park boundary.....	▬ ▪ ▬

Murray

Creek

**VENABLES
VALLEY**

SPENCES
BRIDGE

Arthur Seat

Route Four

Venables Valley

Venables Valley takes its name for Captain Cavendish Venables, who pioneered the area after some uncertainty. Leaving the 74th Highlanders in 1860, he came to the colony of British Columbia and in 1861 secured a military land grant along the trail between Lytton and the Cariboo. He was unable to settle permanently on the land for a few months as the property was reserved by the government while being considered by the Royal Engineers as a possible route for the Cariboo wagon road.

Venables must have been reasonably sure of the outcome, however; by June 1861 Bishop Hills said he had a station here looked after by his "trusty comrade a fine old soldier of the 72nd [sic]. The spot is watered by two lakes connected by a stream and the whole can be irrigated with ease which is of great consequence." Hills remarked of the area that "the graves [near the trails] of this country tell of peril and hardship. There are no old people and rarely a child."

Venables' land lay across an ancient Indian trail, part of the trade route along the Thompson used by the Interior Salish. The trail also led to their bitter-root digging grounds just to the north. When the first white men began to travel through his part of the country it became the main trail north of Lytton.

In 1862 Corporal Robert Howell of the Royal Engineers proposed a route to the east near the present highway. It was a costly venture for the times as a path had to be blasted through Oregon Jack Bluff to the south; however, it eliminated the climb through

Venables Valley and was a more direct line through to 100 Mile Flats beyond Oregon Jack Creek. The decision enabled Captain Venables to establish himself on his claim of 1440 acres.

John "Oregon Jack" Dowling established a wayhouse nearby, close to where the Venables Valley road leaves the highway (mile 96 of the Cariboo Road, as measured from Yale). It was a favorite stopping point for teamsters who had toiled up the long hill from the south.

By the 1870s a wagon road ran through the valley from the mouth of Venables Creek up the slopes and along the valley bottom, winding by the four lakes. It joined with a road up Oregon Jack Creek to the Hat Creek Valley. Eventually the wagon road evolved to a road that serviced ranches, a forestry camp and a couple of mines.

The ranches of Venables and Oregon Jack were bordered by the Basque Ranch, situated between the Cariboo Highway and the Thompson River. The Basque people come from the countryside toward the western end of the Pyrenees Mountains near the Bay of Biscay at the French-Spanish border. The Frenchman who started this ranch, Antoine Minnbarriet, was a Basque. He eventually returned to his homeland but a son of his, Louis Antoine Minnbarriet, stayed to establish his own ranch south of the Venables Valley.

The Venables Valley route for the purpose of this book does not follow the length of the valley as the old road is now impassable from disuse. The new road intersects the valley, creek and old road; continues up to the headwaters of the Venables; then parallels the Twaal Valley as it cuts south to Murray Creek and out to Spences Bridge. The road passes through conifer forests as it winds back towards the logging activity on the Murray Creek watershed. It is a straightforward route, easily travelled in summer months but muddy in wet weather and closed by snows in winter. It is a good area for mountain biking and cross-country skiing.

Maps

National Topographic Series 1:50,000 92I/11 W Ashcroft; 92 I/6 W Spences Bridge, or B.C. Lands & Forest Series 1:25,000 92 I/NW Ashcroft; or 92 I/SW Lytton.

km 0/mi 0   **km 41.8**/mi 26.0

Follow the Cariboo Highway north from Spences Bridge 22.5 kilometres to reach the starting point for this route. Turn west onto the side road, which heads southwesterly. For the first 0.2 kilometres, the road passes through the northwest corner of the Oregon Jack Indian Reserve, bordered by the Thompson River. This land is posted "No trespassing, no shooting."

Year after year, ospreys return to renovate their nests along the Thompson and North Thompson Rivers.

Watch for ospreys — large brown birds with whitish underparts — flying overhead or along the river. A large osprey nest can be seen from the Thompson on the river side of the Basque Ranch. Osprey nests are usually visible from quite a distance, easily recognized by the bulky mass of sticks and branches perched on the top of a standing dead tree. A pair of osprey have been coming to this nest for several years, repairing and adding to it each mating season. It is one of several nests along the Thompson and North Thompson Rivers.

km 1.0/mi 0.6   **km 40.8**/mi 25.4
The road makes a right turn.

km 2.9/mi 1.8   **km 38.9**/mi 24.2
Some alkali ponds can be seen along both sides of the road. These are the Basque salt ponds.

km 3.7/mi 2.3   **km 38.1**/mi 23.7

Epsom salt mine. Alongside the largest of the Basque salt ponds are some old pilings; the bank is stabilized by logs, the site of an old salt mine. A high grade of magnesium sulphate, seen as a whitish coarse-looking salt, is found in crystalline form around the shores and under the murky waters of the ponds. Mining of the salt began in 1919. It is readily soluble in water and has a disagreeable taste. Used medicinally it is usually given in an effervescent solution to make it more palatable. From the mines, the salts were taken to a factory at Ashcroft and shipped out for industrial as well as medicinal uses. Though large deposits remain, it is no longer economically feasible to continue mining.

km 4.7/mi 2.9   **km 37.1**/mi 23.0

Side road left. Private property. This is the old road through Venables Valley. Parts of the road are still used but northern sections are no longer passable.

The best way to see the valley now is on foot. The hike from one end to the other is about 16 kilometres. Walking gives lots of time to enjoy the wild flowers, the old ranch buildings and fences, a gold-molybdenum mine of the 1930s and the rural scenery. Take care to leave all gates along the route as they were found, a courtesy important in any kind of back-country travel.

Continuing the backroad route, go straight and pass the side road into the Venables Valley. White Mountain can be seen ahead.

km 5.1/mi 3.2   **km 36.0**/mi 22.4

Side road. To the right a side road heads north and continues about 1 kilometre to a cattleguard and private property. It passes an old homestead and a hay meadow on the way in. Look for aspen in the valley bottoms and sage on the hills.

km 6.3/mi 3.9   **km 35.5**/mi 22.0

Cattleguard. The road climbs very steeply now, continuing up the headwaters of the Venables.

km 8.5/mi 5.3   **km 33.3**/mi 20.7

Viewpoint. Stop for a moment to take some photos or just to enjoy the view of the Venables Valley below on the left, with the Thompson Valley in the background.

km 9.1/mi 5.7   **km 32.7**/mi 20.3

Cattleguard. The conifer forest through which the road passes is within the Dry Interior Biotic Zone. It is a semi-arid area averaging less than 40 centimetres of rainfall annually, and includes the Okanagan and Similkameen Valleys as well as part of the Thompson. Though the summers are very hot, the winters are surprisingly mild, with minimal snowfalls due to the low precipitation. Since undergrowth is fairly sparse, moving through the forest is not the problem it can be in the Coastal Zone.

Deer are likely to be seen — crossing the road, browsing on the hillsides or around old orchards — by those who travel in the early hours or at dusk. The mule deer inhabits this region, a species that ranges over most of B.C. with the exception of the coastal area and the most northerly parts of the province. Distinguishing characteristics include the large mule-like ears for which it is named, and a white rump patch with a black-tipped, rope-like tail. In the fall, the male or buck grows antlers that form a series of forks. The mule deer has a bounding, stiff-legged gait, and is frequently seen in herds.

The road has levelled out now and leaves the headwaters of the Venables to jump over to the upper reaches of the Twaal.

km 10.1/mi 6.3   **km 31.7**/mi 19.7

Twaal Lake can be seen to the left, surrounded by reeds and decked with pond lilies, both a food source for natives. Cattails have a brown velvetlike seed head, popular with artists and decorators, which disintegrates as the seeds are carried away by the wind. But cattails also have a second way of producing new plants — a creeping root stalk that sends up new shoots each spring. It is the creeping root that was dug up by the Indians and, when dried, ground into flour. The starchy protein roots were quite bland but sometimes were eaten raw or roasted. The long leaves of the cattail were also used by the Indians to weave into mats.

The large seeds of the yellow pond lilies were collected and roasted for food by the Indians. When food was in short supply, the thick root stalk was also used. These roots are enjoyed by black bears too.

km 10.5/mi 6.5   **km 31.3**/mi 19.4

Side road. To the left is a side route through Twaal Creek Valley and the Nicoelton Indian Reserve. The valley, parallel to the Thompson River, was a channel for melting ice at the end of the last ice age. Continue ahead to the right. The NTS 1:50,000 series map, Ashcroft 92 I/11 of 1976, is badly out of date. For the road system here, see the B.C. Department of Lands 1:25,000 series Ashcroft 92 I/NW.

km 10.9/mi 6.8   **km 30.9**/mi 19.2

Junction. The road to the right climbs to Blue Earth Lake, then follows down Blue Earth Creek; it joins up with the Coldwater-Hat Creek Road, which exits south through the Botanie Valley. Maps

Ample clearance and extra horsepower make fording easier.

indicate it also joins the Upper Hat Creek Road but in the spring of 1985 this was barred by a locked gate.

To continue the Venables Route, keep to the left. The road follows along the contours of the hills above the Twaal Valley keeping just to the west of the Indian reserve.

km 12.1/mi 7.5   **km 29.6**/mi 18.4

As the road climbs across the hill, the Twaal Creek road can be seen down in the valley along the reserve's hay meadows.

km 13.7/mi 8.5   **km 28.1**/mi 17.4

After a rocky sidehill is negotiated, the road begins its descent to a creek crossing.

km 14.3/mi 8.9   **km 27.5**/mi 17.1

A dry creek is crossed just upstream of where its waters join with those of the Twaal in wetter seasons.

km 18.0/mi 11.2   **km 23.8**/mi 11.2

There is a final view of the Twaal Creek Valley before the road begins to cut away from the valley and drops down to cross Spence Creek.

km 18.7/mi 11.6   **km 23.1**/mi 14.3

Side road. A road from the headwaters of Spence Creek to the Twaal Valley is crossed just before Spence Creek passes under the main road. Then the road begins a long steep climb. Beware of the roads in this area. In wet weather they become slick very quickly and turn into mud. Before you enter these roads, be well prepared with the equipment mentioned in the appendix of this book.

km 20.3/mi 12.6   **km 21.5**/mi 13.1

Side road. Another road goes left and joins the one mentioned at **km 18.7.** Watch for tiger lilies in the grass beside the road, another of the lilies whose roots were cooked by the Indians and eaten. This lily has maroon-freckled orange blossoms hanging down from a slender stem; it is similar to the garden variety, though smaller.

The road deteriorates for a short distance and then begins to improve as logged areas are passed and more logging side roads are encountered.

km 23.6/mi 14.7   **km 18.2**/mi 11.3

Side road. Keep right where a side road goes off to the left. The left junction meets up with this route again at **km 28.6.**

km 24.5/mi 15.2   **km 17.3**/mi 10.7

A creek crosses under the road and the Murray Valley can be seen ahead. More logging activity is passed as the road gradually descends.

km 26.2/mi 16.3   **km 15.6**/mi 9.7

Another creek crosses under the road.

km 28.0/mi 17.4   **km 13.8**/mi 8.6

Side road. A side track goes off to the right. Keep straight. The leafy bush with the attractive white flowers is ceanothus, a popular plant for deer.

km 28.6/mi 17.8   **km 13.2**/mi 8.2

Junction. Just after another creek is crossed, you reach the junction with the Murray Creek logging road. This junction is the same as **km 52.8** on the Botanie-Murray Creek Route. Refer to it for a description of the road between here and Spences Bridge. Remaining mileages on the Venables Route will include only important junctions. The right road at this point goes west and south through to the Botanie Valley. Keep left for Spences Bridge. Also in this area logging roads fan out on both sides of the Murray Valley.

km 29.3/mi 18.2   **km 12.5**/mi 7.8
Junction. Keep right.

km 31.1/mi 19.3   **km 10.7**/mi 6.6
Side road. Keep straight and continue gradual descent of valley.

km 38.6/mi 24.0   **km 3.2**/mi 2.0
Side road. Keep to the right where a side road goes off to the left to an old homestead.

km 41.4/mi 25.7   **km 0.4**/mi 0.2
Junction. Take a left towards the highway.

km 41.8/mi 26.0   **km 0**/mi 0
Highway 1 at Spences Bridge. To the north is Ashcroft and the Cariboo; to the south is Lytton and the Fraser Canyon. If you can spare a little more time, stop and look around a little more of the country and explore a few more backroads before continuing along the highways to other destinations.

Enjoy backroading at its best when you explore the woods.

Play safe. Cover shaky ground on foot before you drive.

Route Five

Blue Earth Road

Our spring trip into Blue Earth Lake and the road beyond might be described as "a ford too far." It wasn't supposed to be that way; that's just how it turned out. First of all, remember this is supposed to be a semi-arid area with less than 15 inches (40 centimetres) of rain per year. Be that as it may, whenever I head up that way the rain gods deliver a goodly portion of the annual allotment. The creeks rise and road turns to loon-dung: slippery. And if you go down one hill too many, or take one too many fords, you may find yourself at the wrong end of a dead-end one-way road.

On this journey into the junction country my father joined me. We had not had a chance, or had not taken the time, to do much exploring together over the last few years; his retirement and good recovery from heart operations seemed to offer an ideal opportunity.

It was my father who introduced me to wandering these byways. I can remember as a boy driving with him from Vancouver to what seemed like exotic places — Osoyoos, for instance — where a friend of his showed me how to catch a rattlesnake and where we explored for the clay deposits he was interested in. Up the old Cariboo road and over Pavilion mountain, we camped on the roadside, breathed in the sage he so loved and sang as we bounced along in his old Nash (later a Plymouth and even later an early-edition Volkswagen). Somehow he always made me feel that we

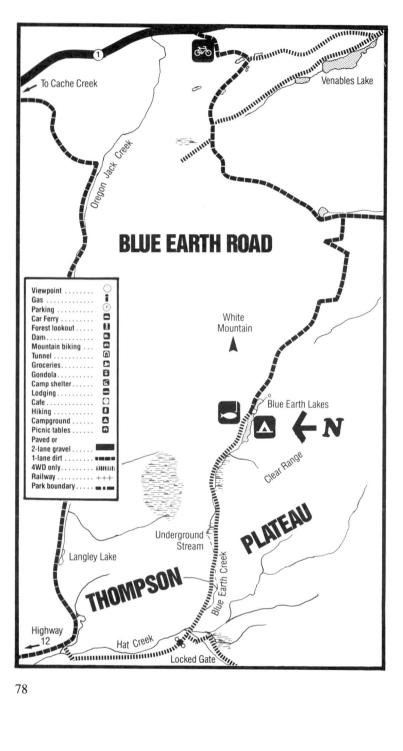

To Cache Creek

Venables Lake

Oregon Jack Creek

BLUE EARTH ROAD

White Mountain

Viewpoint	⊙
Gas	Ⓟ
Parking	🅿
Car Ferry	⛴
Forest lookout	🔭
Dam	🏭
Mountain biking	🚲
Tunnel	🚇
Groceries	🛒
Gondola	🚠
Camp shelter	⛺
Lodging	🛏
Cafe	☕
Hiking	🥾
Campground	🏕
Picnic tables	⛱
Paved or	
2-lane gravel	▬▬▬
1-lane dirt	▬ ▬ ▬
4WD only	‖‖‖‖‖
Railway	+++
Park boundary	▬ ▬ ▬

Blue Earth Lakes

← **N**

Clear Range

PLATEAU

Underground Stream

Langley Lake

THOMPSON

Blue Earth Creek

Highway 12

Hat Creek

Locked Gate

78

were explorers, cowboys or mountain men crossing yet another river or pass. Those times passed and our paths diverged. But as we travelled the first gravel mile of this trip we went back two decades.

For a few days we wandered up backroads, stopped at lakes, talked a lot, made roadside repairs, munched on good fresh lunches, smelled the roses and sage and even plinked with our 22s to prove that our eye was still sharp enough to hit a tin-can lid at 30 paces. And, as with any good backroad trip, we managed to get stuck. On the Blue Earth Road.

We had been aiming for the junction to the Hat Creek Road so we pushed on as the fords became more frequent and the hills steeper. Finally Hat Creek was only 4 km away. It was then we reached the locked gate. We discussed dismantling the fence or breaking the lock but decided there was probably another at the other end and perhaps an irate landowner. So we turned south for Botanie. We would link up with the Laluwissen road that had stopped us a couple of days earlier.

The first ford of Hat Creek could be made only with a salvaged piece of plywood and some old timbers. We bounced across, dismantling our bridge as we went. Then another ford, and another, each more difficult until finally we came to a deep rough crossing of Hat Creek with a steep hill on the other side.

The ford was rough enough — the kind where you hear rocks hitting the undercarriage — but the real problem was the hill. Not only was it slippery, but my van has always had a dislike of high altitudes — and we were around 6000 feet. Halfway up the slippery hill it powered out and started sliding back towards the ford like the beginning of a luge run. I tried again, and again. Finally we admitted defeat and turned around. With only a little difficulty we arrived back at the locked gate, reiterated our arguments, cursed the rancher and turned right. We had two hours of light left and a couple of tricky hills.

Everything went okay until I tried to dodge a fallen tree. The back end skated free and slipped to the right, narrowly missed a tree, nailed a stump...and the back wheel dropped off the road. We were stuck, 25 kilometres from the nearest help. Or the nearest doctor. Bypass, pacemaker, nitro pills? " The doctor says my heart is better than new. I can do whatever I want." I hoped he was right.

Basically our solution was simple, but called for a certain amount of work. We had two jack-all jacks so we jacked up the rear end in stages and built a new road under it, at the same time using another to pull the van sideways. It worked, but it took two hours. And the doctor was right. Dad could do whatever he had a mind to.

The sky was darkening when we hit the next trouble area. One hundred yards of mud on an uphill grade and we bogged down with a sickening whump. Somehow I got it to back up. We dragged over all the fallen lodgepole pine and branches we could find and laid them in the muddy ruts. Maybe if we could keep the van away from the mud that grabbed at the underchassis we would make it.

In a tree-crashing and branch-tossing run I lurched 10 feet farther. Time to camp, I suggested. Maybe it would dry out overnight. If not I would walk out for help. It seemed the best plan or the only plan. But I did not like the idea of leaving Dad on his own and the walk would be a long one. He suggested one more try. After a half-hour of discussion I agreed.

I gave the van a pep talk; Dad walked, I buckled up and put the pedal to the metal. Bouncing and slewing sideways we careened to the top of the hill. "By God, I wish I had that on film," Dad laughed as he puffed up to me, popping a pill in his mouth. That was the last of the hills. We agreed we should be okay now.

At Blue Earth Lake we met some other campers. Help would have been closer than we thought. Then the first raindrops hit our windshield. Fifteen minutes later it began to rain, hard, and by the time we reached the Venables Valley Road we could not see the road for the torrent. The road was awash. We hit the highway at 11 p.m. in a blinding storm and retreated to Cache Creek. "See," I said, "I told you it would dry up."

Maps

National Togographic Series 1:50,000 92I/11 Ashcroft; 92 I/12, 92 I/6 Spences Bridge, or B.C. Lands & Forest Series 1:25,000 92 I/NW Ashcroft.

Note: the best map for this route is the 1:250,000 92 I/NW. The 1:50,000 series are out of date and do not show the Venables Valley roads in their present location. On the 1:50,000 series two routes are indicated into Blue Earth Lakes. Only the northerly one over the ridge is passable.

km 0/mi 0

The starting point for this route is the Venables Valley Road. For details of the first 10 kilometres see that route. Follow the Cariboo Highway north from Spences Bridge 22.5 kilometres to the Venables road. Turn west onto the side road which heads in southwest. For the first 0.2 kilometres the road passes through the northwest corner of the Oregon Jack Indian Reserve.

The reserve is named for John "Oregon Jack" Dowling who established a wayhouse near here. (See introduction to Route Four.)

Family evenings by the campfire brought back many memories along the Blue Earth Road.

km 1.0/mi 0.6

The road makes a right turn.

km 2.9/mi 1.8

Some alkali ponds can be seen along both sides of the road. These are the Basque salt ponds.

km 3.7/mi 2.3

Epsom salt mine. Alongside the largest of the Basque salt ponds are some old pilings, the remnants of an old salt mine begun in 1919. The road continues its gradual climb up the hillside.

km 4.7/mi 2.9

Side road left. Private property. This is the old road through Venables Valley, originally an Indian trail, part of the trade route along the Thompson used by the Interior Salish. After the valley was eliminated as a possible route for the Cariboo wagon road in 1862, Captain Venables settled here and by the 1870s a wagon road ran through the valley from the mouth of Venables Creek along the Venables Valley to join with a road up Oregon Jack Creek to the Hat Creek Valley. Parts of the road are still used but the northern sections are no longer passable.

Continue straight ahead, passing the side road into the Venables Valley. White Mountain can be seen ahead.

km 5.1/mi 3.2

Side road. To the right a side road heads north and continues about 1 kilometre to a cattleguard and private property.

km 6.3/mi 3.9

Cattleguard. The road climbs very steeply now, continuing up the headwaters of the Venables.

km 8.5/mi 5.3

Viewpoint. Stop for a moment to take some photos or just to enjoy the view of the Venables Valley below on the left, with the Thompson Valley in the background.

km 9.1/mi 5.7

Cattleguard. The conifer forest through which the road passes is within the Dry Interior Biotic Zone. It is a semi-arid area averaging less than 40 centimetres of rainfall annually, and includes the Okanagan and Similkameen Valleys as well as part of the Thompson.

The road levels out and leaves the headwaters of the Venables to cross over to the upper reaches of the Twaal.

km 10.1/mi 6.3

Twaal Lake can be seen to the left, surrounded by reeds and decked with pond lilies.

km 10.5/mi 6.5

Side road. To the left is a side route through Twaal Creek Valley and the Nicoelton Indian Reserve. The valley, parallel to the Thompson River, was a channel for melting ice at the end of the last ice age. Continue ahead to the right.

km 10.9/mi 6.8

Junction. The road to the left continues south to the Murray Creek exit of the Botanie Valley road, eventually reaching the highway at Spences Bridge. The right fork climbs to Blue Earth Lake, then follows down Blue Earth Creek, eventually joining up with the Coldwater-Hat Creek road that exits south through the Botanie Valley. Maps indicate it also joins the Upper Hat Creek Road but in the spring of 1985 this was closed with a locked gate. Take the right fork.

km 11.0/mi 6.8

Twaal Lake and Murray Creek road down to left. The road climbs a shoulder of White Mountain from 3500 feet (1067 metres) in the valley to a ridge pass at 4800 feet (1463 metres).

km 11.7/mi 7.3

A side road goes down to left. The main road is in good condition, suitable for most vehicles through to the lakes.

km 13.4/mi 8.3

An unmapped logging road goes to the right as we reach the pass.

km 13.5/mi 8.4

Cattleguard.

km 14.3/mi 8.9

Creek crossing. Two nice mule deer bounded across the road here.

km 15.5/mi 9.6

A track goes to the right, destination unknown.

km 16.5/mi 10.3

A creek drops down from White Mountain.

km 16.7/mi 10.4

A track to the right bypasses this main road and rejoins at **km 17.6.**

km 18.1/mi 11.2

An unnamed lake can be seen down to left. It is separated from Blue Earth by only a few metres.

km 18.4/mi 11.4

Junction. Turn left to reach the lake shore and the BCFS Blue Earth Lake recreation site. Trout spawning. A Fish and Wildlife Branch sign here warns: *Anglers. This lake contains only trout. Please keep it that way. The transport of live fish and the use of such for bait is illegal and can result in spoiled trout fishing.*

In other information the branch explains that coarse fish in the wrong place are a menace to quality sport fishing. When it comes to reproducing, shiners, suckers, carp, squawfish, sculpin, chub and their like far outstrip the trout family. Transferred to game-fish water, they take over. Some of them prey on fry and eggs; all of them compete with game fish for food and living space. For major fisheries there is no remedy. Rotenone, employed to clean out coarse fish, is too expensive for use in any but the smallest lakes.

Careless transfers of coarse fish jeopardize the hatchery system that supplies six to seven million game fish annually to more than 500 B.C. lakes. Hatcheries get 95 per cent of their egg supply from wild fish. Forty per cent come from one lake. If a key lake is lost to coarse fish the sport fishing in many stocked lakes will decline.

"No Trespassing" signs pop up in some unexpected places, but it doesn't pay to ignore them.

Transfers of coarse fish result from anglers illegally using "live minnows" for bait, from children at play and from people unaware of the consequences.

The Fish and Wildlife Branch warns that the transfer of live fish is illegal. If you see live fish being moved from one body of water to another, or being used as live bait, report as soon as possible to the nearest Conservation Officer, Branch office or call Zenith 2235, toll free, 24 hours, 7 days a week.

A small well-used cabin at this east end of Blue Earth has a history of fishing expeditions tattooed on its walls: *Gerry W. and Dianne W. was here July 12 1984. Good fishing. 7 in 1¹/₂ hours. Worm and marshmellow. 2 - 3¹/₄ lbs. July 19 & 20 19 small ones.*

When we were here in May the creek was alive with spawning trout and loons sat expectantly offshore.

Beyond the lake junction the road skirts along the high bank above the lake. It is not suitable for trailers or vehicles without high clearance. In wet weather 4x4s will likely be necessary. Reaching the Botanie Valley by this route involves several fords and some steep grades.

Ahead is a beautiful view of the lake and an alpine area. The mountain back at left is Lookout Point, 6620 feet (2018 metres).

km 18.4/mi 11.4
A cattleguard for Wagner Creek Ranch.

km 21.7/mi 13.5
As the road passes some beaver ponds it becomes rough and slippery.

84

km 22.9/mi 14.2

The road crosses Blue Earth Creek but usually the creek is not evident as for a short distance it flows underground. In the meadow the road is just a track. After the crossing is a steep climb to a wooded ridge.

km 26.7/mi 16.6

The road leaves the timber for a meadow where it fords Blue Earth Creek — suddenly resurfaced. The meadow appears to have been part of an old homestead as there are remains of a cabin with scattered household debris.

km 27/mi 16.8

Another ford of an unnamed tributary of Hat Creek.

km 27.4/mi 17.0

Junction. Left is the route up Hat Creek and down North Laluwissen Creek to the Botanie Valley and Lytton. To the right is the road to Upper Hat Creek. Unfortunately there is a new fence and locked gate just 100 metres down the road, and a "NO TRESPASSING" sign. The legality of locking a public-access road is debatable; however, locked it is. The road south to the Botanie is more difficult than the road back to Blue Earth. This junction is at an elevation of 4000 feet (1219 metres) and climbs to 5500 feet (1676 metres) at the pass to Laluwissen.

km 28.0/mi 17.4

Ford of Hat Creek. Again the topo sheet in the NTS 1:50,000 series, Lillooet 92 I/12, seems to be in error. We could not make the fords shown on the map coincide with those on the creek.

km 30.5/mi 20.0

A fence and another ford of Hat Creek. This one is deep and 30 feet wide, followed by a hill (slippery when wet) on the far side.

km 31.0/mi 19.3

Another ford of Hat Creek, again followed by a hill.

km 31.8/mi 19.8

At the junction of Hat Creek and an unnamed tributary there is another ford, followed by a long steep section. For us it was the end of the road. The ford is (or was) rough and the drizzle that was welcoming spring made the road too slippery for our two-wheel drive to climb. A 4x4 should have no trouble continuing. Our only choice was to return via Blue Earth, which was only just possible. It should only be another two kilometres to the pass and then one or two to the described section of the Botanie Road.

A buddy can help you improvise your way out of the gumbo. That's my son Richard on the business end of the shovel.

The road takes a turn for the better as we head towards Big Bar near the Fraser.

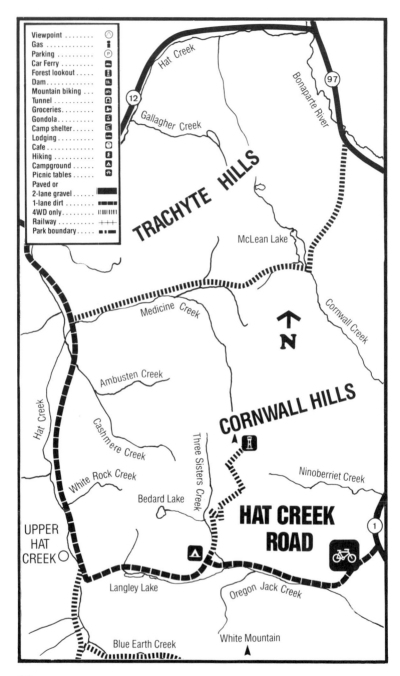

Viewpoint . . . . ⊘
Gas . . . . ℹ
Parking . . . . Ⓟ
Car Ferry . . . .
Forest lookout . . . . .
Dam . . . .
Mountain biking . . .
Tunnel . . . .
Groceries . . . .
Gondola . . . .
Camp shelter . . . . . .
Lodging . . . .
Cafe . . . .
Hiking . . . .
Campground . . . . . . ▲
Picnic tables . . . . . .
Paved or
2-lane gravel . . . . .
1-lane dirt . . . .
4WD only . . . .
Railway . . . . +++
Park boundary . . . . .

TRACHYTE HILLS

Hat Creek

Gallagher Creek

12

Bonaparte River

97

McLean Lake

Medicine Creek

Cornwall Creek

↑N

Ambusten Creek

Hat Creek

Cashmere Creek

White Rock Creek

Three Sisters Creek

CORNWALL HILLS

Ninoberriet Creek

Bedard Lake

HAT CREEK ROAD

1

UPPER HAT CREEK ○

Langley Lake

Oregon Jack Creek

Blue Earth Creek

White Mountain ▲

88

Route Six

Hat Creek Valley

Geological processes are generally very slow in human terms so that, apart from catastrophic incidents, changes are almost imperceptible within a lifetime. Most of the obvious changes in landscape result from the impact of people and the utilization of natural resources, especially in the production of energy. Upper Hat Creek is a potential source of thermal energy because of its large coal deposits; should it be mined for this use, the valley will certainly change.

Hat Creek Valley is now known to have two major coal deposits, and may be the largest coal reserve in the world. A deposit at the north end of the valley has been noted for a long time and surface coal was used by some of the early settlers for fuel. A more recent discovery is a coal deposit in the centre of the valley, found during test drilling within the past four years.

B.C. Hydro is continuing its studies of the feasibility of open pit mining of the coal to fuel a power plant, amidst great controversy from:
- some of the valley's residents who do not wish to see their homes replaced by a crater estimated to become 11 kilometres in circumference by 0.3 kilometres deep;
- environmentalists with concerns about the contamination of Hat Creek and the Fraser River drainage system, about the low heat value of the coal and its high ash content, and about contamination of the air from hazardous trace elements; and
- scientists who feel that the lignite coal could be better used as an environmental cleaning agent.

The above views were expressed in the original edition of this volume in 1979. Much has changed in the valley since then.

B.C. Hydro has now spent close to $75 million in studies leading to a proposal for a $1.5 billion thermal plant here. While the studies showed that there are indeed two massive coal deposits beneath the rangeland, the project was put on the back burner — to the relief of many. In the meantime, however, 6000 tonnes of low grade coal had been mined, leaving large scars on the Hat Creek Valley hillsides. Elsewhere in the valley large dumps of coal and old drilling sites are evidence of the exploration. Enjoy the vistas of ranchland here; if the project is ever reinstated, the valley will be unrecognizable.

The Upper Hat Creek Route begins at the Cariboo Highway and follows up Oregon Jack Creek and through the Upper Hat Creek Valley to Highway 12, giving an opportunity to see the valley as it is now. Most of the country along the route is ranch country, so hay meadows, ranch building, cattle, cattleguards and open fields are part of the scenery. There are also ducks to be seen, and beaver ponds and deer. A side road near the headwaters of Oregon Jack climbs up to Cornwall Mountain Lookout and some of the finest meadows of alpine flowers that can be reached by road. In the heat of summer, the mountains also provide respite from the furnacelike heat of the valley bottoms.

The road should present little problem in dry weather and the Hat Creek section is usually passable all year round. The only problem we encountered was some mud on Cornwall Mountain just beyond the forestry lookout tower, and it could be avoided by turning back at the lookout. However, cars with low clearance would be best to avoid the Oregon Jack portion of the road, gaining access and egress at Highway 12.

Maps

National Topographic Series 1:50,000 92 I/11 W Ashcroft; 92 I/12 E Lillooet; 92 I/13 E Pavilion or B.C. Lands & Forest Series 1:125,000 92 I/NW Ashcroft.

km 0/mi 0   **km 42.2**/mi 26.2

North of Spences Bridge about 38 kilometres along the Cariboo Highway, a side road takes off to the west. Follow this road, which (a sign indicates) leads to Cornwall Mountain Lookout.

On the far side of the highway from where the road turns off is a low hill known as Red Hill. The red tones in the rock accounting for its name are caused by iron compounds. East of Red Hill is the Black Canyon on the Thompson River, a narrowing of the watercourse as it passes through the vertical black walls in large whirlpools.

A bald eagle is often seen soaring above the canyon or perched high on the scarp, near a nest of sticks on the cliff ledge. Even from

Coyotes didn't linger at Ashcroft Manor on those long-gone days when the Cornwall brothers pursued them with foxhounds.

a considerable distance the adult bald eagle can be recognized by its large size and white head and tail contrasting with its black-looking (actually dark brown) body. The bird has become a symbol of freedom, and the national emblem of the United States of America. We might remember that Benjamin Franklin suggested the wild turkey.

km 0.5/mi 0.3   **km 41.7**/mi 25.9

The road climbs slowly, passing around a feedlot — a supplement form of nourishment to the grasslands that are the primary food source for cattle in Cariboo country.

The hillside sagebrush is an invader species, moving in when soil is very poor or when grass is overgrazed. Though cowboys and sagebrush have become synonymous, the sage actually came after the cattle chewed the bunchgrass down to its roots. Its narrow leaves have three rounded points or teeth by which the shrub can be identified and which give the plant its Latin name of *Artemisia tridentata*. The smell of the plant is familiar to those who have travelled through the dry interior country. It was grown in English gardens for its aroma, used by the Blackfeet Indians in the Sun Dance ceremony, and used elsewhere to make liquor, medicine, tea and (of course) a spice. Try a few wild leaves. Sage has also been recommended as a substitute for mothballs because of its strong smell.

km 1.0/mi 0.6   **km 41.2**/mi 25.6

Ashcroft Manor. The green fields in the distance are Ashcroft Manor and Cornwall Flats. In 1859 two brothers, Henry Penant Cornwall and Clement Fitzalan Cornwall, came via Pemberton Meadows and Pavilion Mountain into the bunchgrass flats above the Thompson River. After building a cabin for the winter they decided to stay and establish a ranch and roadside stopping-place. They named the ranch Ashcroft Manor after the family home in Gloucestershire, England. Among their enterprises was a lumber mill using Cornwall Creek as a source of power, a flour mill and a ranch. They also introduced hunting with hounds to the area, attracting many visitors to the annual "coyote hunts." One of the brothers, Clement, was Lieutenant-Governor of B.C. from 1881 to 1886.

This stretch of land to the north and northwest was in use long before ranchers came to the area, though, for it is the traditional bitter-root digging grounds of the Interior Salish Indians. They collected the roots when the flower was in bloom, usually in early May, combing the territory between Oregon Jack Creek north to Rattlesnake Hill, on the far side of the Bonaparte. As an edible root it was second in importance only to the camas, with balsam root of third importance, followed by tiger lily, glacier lily and chocolate lily.

The Indian name for the plant is speetlum or spatlum, bitter-root being the white man's label; even after the extremely bitter orange skin was peeled off, the white root retained a grapefruitlike tartness. The Latin name *Lewisia rediviva* refers to the fact that the plant was collected by Captain Merriweather Lewis of the historic Lewis and Clark expedition and sent to the botanist Pursh; the dried plant was replanted by the botanist and surprisingly grew, resulting in the species being named "come to life again."

km 2.7/mi 1.0   **km 39.5**/mi 24.5

Open fields give way to coniferous forest, a good place to see birds in the trees bordering the grassy meadows. On more than one occasion we have observed red crossbills (which have the unusual characteristic of being able to breed at any time of the year), shrikes, which are songbirds as well as predators, and waxwings, crested birds with sleek painted-looking feathers.

km 3.7/mi 2.3   **km 38.5**/mi 23.9

At this point the road begins to follow Oregon Jack Creek, a tributary of the Thompson River that rises in the southern Cornwall Hills. Oregon Jack was an early settler named Jack Dowling who moved into the area in 1862, having come from Oregon. He later ran a small hotel, gaining a reputation as a drinking man but nevertheless a popular host.

km 5.5/mi 3.4   **km 36.7**/mi 22.8

Cattleguard.

km 5.9/mi 3.7   **km 36.3**/mi 22.5

Between the road and Oregon Jack Creek is a small homestead.

km 9.8/mi 6.1   **km 32.4**/mi 20.1

Passing into fir forest, the road continues its gradual climb through ranch properties and a small Indian reserve. Wild rose bushes growing along the wayside add to the scene at any time of year, and when in blossom give off a lovely fragrance.

km 11.3/mi 7.0   **km 30.9**/mi 19.2

Lun D Ranch. It is difficult to pass the Lun D Ranch without smiling after reading the advice posted there: "Don't just sit there, nag your husband." Across the road from the ranch gate is a rock cliff; beyond, the road becomes rougher. The purple or mauve rockery plant growing on the cliffs is penstemon.

km 13.4/mi 8.3   **km 28.8**/mi 17.9

Junction. The road to the right climbs about 8.7 kilometres up to Cornwall Mountain forestry lookout. The view, alpine meadows and fresh mountain air make it a great destination. The mountain, of course, is named for the Cornwall brothers who, as already mentioned, established Ashcroft Manor.

My first visit to the alpine meadows of Cornwall Mountain was a good lesson in the differences noticed in a change of altitude of 1700 metres. We left the Cariboo Highway feeling ill from the July mid-day heat; yet on the mountain the temperature was pleasantly cool. This fact was appreciated by other creatures as well, including the mosquitos that were in abundance on the mountain-top. Because of the altitude the flowers were at a peak in July, and the conifers were still in the flower stage, long past in the valley below.

It was easy to find a camping spot surrounded by flowers, with a wonderful view and a perfect sunset to end the day. A word of caution here, though: take great care when visiting the alpine area. The environment is so fragile that tire marks or careless steps can leave scars for a very long time. Keep vehicles on the road and camp where tents and footsteps will not damage the plants. You will also need to bring your own water up the mountain and carry out all garbage.

Another highlight of our short stay on Cornwall was chatting over coffee with forestry lookout ranger Wade Collins. At the time of our visit, he had been manning the lookout for ten years, making it his home from June to September during the fire-hazard season. He explained how his equipment was used and talked of the trend to close many of the lookouts in favor of air surveillance. When we bogged down in some muddy ruts on the road he obligingly offered to help us out.

The colorful flowers on the mountain are too varied for a complete list. They included the following, on the floor of the aspen forest and in the alpine meadows: larkspur, dandelion, cinquefoil, Indian paintbrush, yarrow, avens, shooting star, penstemon, wild rose, clover vetch, thistle, sticky geranium, lupine and balsam root. Deer tracks were seen around the lookout, and chipmunks in the trees down the road. On the way back, watch for views of the surrounding country, including Bedard Lake and Venables Lake.

Back at the **km 13.4** junction, take a left off Oregon Jack Road to continue through Hat Creek: that is, a right turn on coming down from the lookout.

The BCFS Three Sisters Recreation Site is located near this junction, named for the creek that flows from Cornwall Mountain. It is a small site with good drinking water and receives light use. There are toilets.

km 14.6/mi 9.1   **km 27.6**/mi 17.1
Cattleguard. The road continues downhill.

km 16.2/mi 10.1   **km 26.0**/mi 16.1
A beaver pond below the road is the first of a series of ponds and swamps parallelling the road on the left.

km 17.9/mi 11.1   **km 24.3**/mi 15.1
A large beaver pond lies to the left, surrounded by willow and aspen groves. Watch for deer along here. Our journey included the view of a lone mule deer browsing in the swamp. After we had observed him for a few minutes and taken a few photos, he detected our presence and bounded off in graceful leaps.

The yellow flower that looks like a sparsely petalled dandelion is called salsify, oyster plant or goat's beard. After it was introduced to this continent from Africa and Eurasia, the Indians used the thick root as a food. The seed head resembles that of a giant dandelion, and reveals intriguing patterns through a camera lens or other magnifying glass.

km 18.8/mi 11.7   **km 23.4**/mi 14.5
Hay meadows lie around the ponds and Langley Lake. Ditches occasionally can be seen, draining the hay meadows. There is another cabin here, and a rock bluff to the right.

km 20.6/mi 12.8   **km 21.6**/mi 13.4
Cattleguard.

km 21.9/mi 13.6   **km 20.3**/mi 12.6
Hat Creek Valley stretches out to the north as we approach the first of the many ranch properties checking the valley. Hat Creek, which flows north through the valley and then east in the Bonaparte, was formerly called Riviere aux Chapeaux; it derives its name from an Indian village with a large granite boulder nearby containing several hatlike cavities.

km 22.4/mi 13.9   **km 19.8**/mi 12.3
Cattleguard.

km 22.7/mi 14.1   **km 19.5**/mi 12.1
Junction. The road to the left leads past an old log barn and corrals; jogging left a second time, it goes south through to the Blue Earth road that exits via the Venables Valley, or continues along North Laluwissen to Botanie Valley as detailed in the Botanie Route. On last inspection the gate to this forest road was locked. See Blue Earth Creek Road for a further description. Keep right at the junction to continue through the Hat Creek Valley.

km 23.0/mi 14.3   **km 19.2**/mi 11.9
Cattleguard.

km 23.5/mi 14.6   **km 18.7**/mi 11.6
Upper Hat Creek. A ranch road goes off to the left. Rockhounds may be interested to know that jasper-agate occurs on the ridge up to the east. On a recent visit to the Cache Creek and Hat Creek area, geologists studied the cherts there and estimated deposits to be about 225 million years old, having been left on a ridge under the Pacific Ocean that gradually uplifted to become part of North America. Chert and jasper are both forms of cryptocrystalline quartz: that is, quartz with microscopic crystals.

km 24.5/mi 15.2   **km 17.7**/mi 11.0
Gordon Parke Ranch. In 1862, Philip Parke arrived in the colony of British Columbia after leaving his home in Northern Ireland lured by tales of the gold rush. On his way to the interior he met so

Another ford. Practice makes perfect with these.

many unsuccessful miners that he decided to homestead. After working in the Ashcroft-Cache Creek area to raise some money, he settled down to raise cattle on the Bonaparte Ranch.

Management of the ranch was taken over by a nephew, Henry Farqueson Parke, who had also emigrated from Northern Ireland. Henry with his Irish wife and four children wintered at a ranch house near Cache Creek and would go up to "the meadows" at Upper Hat Creek and camp out for the summer and put up the hay. The ranch was later divided into two ranches by Alan and Gordon Parke. The first log home was built on the Hat Creek property in 1912.

km 26.4/mi 16.4   **km 15.8**/mi 9.8
  Allan Pocock Ranch.

km 28.8/mi 17.9   **km 13.4**/mi 8.3
  Drill site. An earth-pile near the road was one of the test sites in the valley for Hat Creek coal.

km 29.1/mi 18.1   **km 13.1**/mi 8.1
Upper Hat Creek Ranch.

km 32.2/mi 20.0   **km 10.0**/mi 6.2
After passing another of the small alkaline lakes or potholes that attract passing waterfowl, we cross Ambusten Creek.

km 34.1/mi 21.1   **km 8.1**/mi 5.0
Cattleguard.

km 36.5/mi 22.7   **km 5.7**/mi 3.5
Medicine Creek crosses under the road to join Hat Creek, having drained some of the north slopes of the Cornwall Hills. A road goes east up Medicine Creek over a ridge to McLean Lake, an Indian reserve, and exits through the Bonaparte Reserve on Highway 97 a few miles north of Cache Creek.

km 39.4/mi 24.5   **km 2.8**/mi 1.7
A side road goes back to the left, following the west side of Hat Creek for a short distance.

km 39.9/mi 24.8   **km 2.3**/mi 1.4
Cattleguard. Some old buildings are passed and then a bridge crosses over Hat Creek. Note the flume for irrigation.

km 40.7/mi 25.3   **km 1.5**/mi 0.9
A private road takes off to the left, a back lane to many of the Hat Creek properties.

km 42.2/mi 26.2   **km 0**/mi 0
Highway 12. Here we have a choice of directions at the end of the Upper Hat Creek Route.
A right turn on Highway 12 follows Hat Creek for about 21 kilometres to meet the Cariboo Highway at Carquille, where Hat Creek post was run by the Hudson's Bay Company for many years. When the Cariboo Road came through, Hat Creek House was built as a stage stop. Although on private property, the historic building is being restored and will one day be open to public tours. It is worth a visit.
A left turn on Highway 12 goes 60 kilometres to Lillooet, passing Pavilion Lake and Marble Canyon Park, through Pavilion and along the east bank of the Fraser River. Near Pavilion there is also a road up over Pavilion Mountain, a route detailed next as the Cariboo Road, Lillooet to Clinton. The choice is yours.

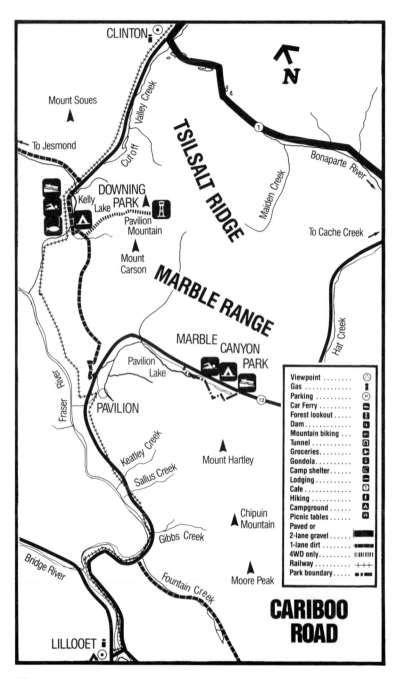

CLINTON

Mount Soues

To Jesmond

TSILSALT RIDGE

Valley Creek

Cut off

Maiden Creek

Bonaparte River

To Cache Creek

Kelly Lake

DOWNING PARK

Pavilion Mountain

Mount Carson

MARBLE RANGE

Fraser River

Pavilion Lake

MARBLE CANYON PARK

PAVILION

Keatley Creek

Sallus Creek

Mount Hartley

Hat Creek

Chipuin Mountain

Gibbs Creek

Bridge River

Fountain Creek

Moore Peak

Viewpoint	⊘
Gas	⛽
Parking	Ⓟ
Car Ferry	⛴
Forest lookout	🔭
Dam	🚧
Mountain biking . . .	🚲
Tunnel	🚇
Groceries	🛒
Gondola	🚡
Camp shelter	⛺
Lodging	🏠
Cafe	☕
Hiking	🥾
Campground	⛺
Picnic tables	⛱
Paved or 2-lane gravel	▬▬
1-lane dirt	▬ ▬
4WD only	‖‖‖‖
Railway	+++
Park boundary	■·■·■

CARIBOO ROAD

LILLOOET

Route Seven

Cariboo Road

The original Cariboo Road began at Lillooet, the terminus of the Douglas or Harrison-Lillooet Trail from the coast. The road was surveyed in 1861 and by the end of that year contractor Gustavus Blin Wright had completed the 47-mile section from Lillooet over Pavilion Mountain and through Cutoff Valley to Clinton.

Every mile was important in the days of travelling by wagon and on foot, so mileposts were placed along the route indicating the distance from Lillooet. Markers were 12 to 14 inch squared timbers with roofed tops to shed the rain. Roadhouses, some still operating today, provided meals and accommodation and took their names from the mileposts. The Lillooet-Clinton section of the wagon road was the main route to the Cariboo until 1863, when the Yale-Cariboo wagon road was built.

More than a centry later this same route can still be followed by a road slightly straightened and improved yet essentially the same. Even the countryside has changed very little through the years. True, the towns of Lillooet and Clinton have mellowed since their wild frontier days but still function as supply points and stopping-places for travellers. Between these two communities the back-roader will find panoramic views of the Fraser River and benchlands, Indian villages, irrigated ranchlands, a general store at Pavilion with the flavor of days gone by, steep grades on Pavilion Mountain and a historic ranch nestled on the mountain.

The gravel roads at both ends of the route are straightforward and should cause no difficulty. However, the section that traverses Pavilion Mountain switchbacks up and drops steeply down on the precipitous north side. It would be passable for regular passenger cars in summer weather, but should be avoided in heavy rains or snow. Until the road was widened, cars had to back up at every curve to maneuver around the sharp zigzags. It is not suitable for trailers.

In its early days, Lillooet was known as Cayoosh. According to the Victoria *Colonist,* "The town was named by Chief Justice Begbie, from a tribe of Indians known as the Cayooshes, during his first visit to the locality in the Spring of 1859." Another story says that Cayoosh Flats was so named when the body of a Cayuse or Indian pony was found in the river nearby.

Whatever the case may be, the name was changed again in 1860 - to Lillooet, since it was situated at the end of the trail from Lillooet Lake to the Fraser. There is some confusion as well about the meaning of the word Lillooet. It is the name of an Indian tribe and is thought to be from an Indian word meaning wild onion. Another possible source is the Squamish word for "end of the trail."

In the winter of 1861, the population was estimated to be "about 350 souls, most of whom are wintering there with the intention of starting for the upper country as soon as the first sign of a 'break up' in the cold weather is given." By 1863 the number of people in Lillooet had swelled to 15,000, the second largest city north of Frisco. The town boasted 13 saloons and 25 other liquor outlets. In October of that year, "The place was full of miners, on their way down to Victoria for the winter. Drinking and card playing went on until long after midnight, amid a constant string of oaths and miners' slang."

Lillooet's economy slumped a few years later when the Yale section of the Cariboo Road opened, but things picked up with the discovery of gold at the Golden Cache on Cayoosh Creek and the Lorne discovery up the Bridge River. The population, no longer dependent on gold, is now about 6500 and residents are employed in a diverse group of industries centred around natural resources.

Lillooet offers visitors the usual hotels, motels, restaurants and a campground, with the added attractions of a good local museum and historical society. There are several attractions worth walking to such as the "Hanging Tree" where several lawbreakers are said to have been strung up before the coming of Judge Begbie's law.

Rockhounds will be interested in searching for jade, aided by directions from one of the many local rock shops. The hunting in the area is good; anglers can fish for rainbow trout or massive

Fording a stream may look easy. A few minutes of scouting, though, can spare you hours of grief.

Fraser River sturgeon, which reach lengths over 13 feet and weigh in at 530 pounds. Sturgeon fishermen will need special gear and would do well to check at sporting-goods stores for the names of local guides who will supply gear and river transportation to the best river bars.

Whatever your interest, Lillooet is a good place to begin the explorations of area backroads. For other roads, see Vol. 1 in this series, *Bridge River Country.*

Maps

National Topographic Series 1:50,000 92I/12W Lillooet; 92 I/13 W Pavilion; 92 P/4 Clinton; 92 P/4 E Clinton or B.C. Lands and Forests Series 1:25,000 92 I/NW Ashcroft; 92 P/SW Bonaparte Lake.

km 0/mi 0   **km 72.5**/mi 45.0

The route begins, as did the historic trail, in what is now the centre of Lillooet. The Mile Zero cairn is built of stones taken from the many piles of tailings gravel left after the river was placer-mined. All along the Fraser, mounds of rock are still in evidence. Some of the miners found the gold they were searching for just one mile below town, near the mouth of Cayoosh Creek, where over $3 million in gold is said to have been taken out.

Head south along the main street, across the railway tracks past the 1920s railway station and down the hill to the Bridge of the 23 Camels. There is a plaque at this western end, which reads:

The Bridge of the 23 Camels. So named to commemorate British Columbia's first - and last - experience with camels, 23 of which were imported in 1862 by John Callbreath of Seton Portage to pack supplies from Lillooet to the Upper Cariboo. The experiment failed when the Bactrian Camels were found to frighten horses, domestic stock and even humans. They were turned loose and most were never seen again. A few survived and the last died in 1905 after many years as a ranch pet.

The bridge was dedicated in September 1980.

km 1.4/mi 0.9   **km 71.1**/mi 44.1

Junction with Highway 12. Take the left fork for the Cariboo Road route.

A right turn onto Highway 12 heads down the east bank of the Fraser to its confluence with the Thompson River at Lytton. The land just south of this point was a Japanese settlement, known as East Lillooet, during the Second World War. Long-standing prejudice against the Japanese people was intensified by the attack on Pearl Harbour on December 7, 1941, and resulted in one of the federal government's infamous declarations under the War Measures Act. All Japanese people were to be evacuated from a "protected area" 100 miles between the coast waters and the Cascade Mountains, including those who were Canadian-born. In 1942 between March and October, 20,000 Japanese were taken from the settlements of the Lower Mainland and relocated.

The town of Lillooet did not allow any Japanese people to live there, but one of the self-supporting settlements was located at East Lillooet. Evacuees built tarpaper shacks and a school building that doubled as a community hall. They worked on their vegetable plots, using water pumped up from the Fraser River for irrigation; brought in drinking water from the PGE station, or melted snow in winter; and they cut firewood. Eventually their activities broadened to include a sawmill, a farming co-operative and a cannery.

After the ban was lifted, the Japanese people moved away. A few went back to Japan, but most spread out through the interior of B.C. and to the coast to become integrated into the cosmopolitan population of British Columbia. The tarpaper houses were sold for $10 to $25 and the schoolhouse was sold for the lumber. Now all that remains in the area are a few foundations, an airstrip and a rodeo ground.

For the Cariboo Road take a left turn on Highway 12.

km 2.4/mi 1.5   **km 70.1**/mi 43.5

A stop-of-interest sign:

Lillooet. Here was the gateway to gold! Yellow gold-lined bars of the Fraser and beyond was the lure of the Cariboo. Like a magnet it drew thousands of miners on the long Harrison Trail [Douglas Trail] through the Coast Mountains. From this focal point the first Cariboo Wagon Road was started northward in 1858. The trail end at Lillooet became mile 0 on the new road to riches.

When Cayoose was booming in 1860 there was another town on this east side of the river, known as Nicokoniana, or to the Americans as Parsonville. It was named for a U.S. storekeeper who built the first house here. This settlement was the actual Mile Zero of the Cariboo Road.

km 3.8/mi 2.4   **km 68.7**/mi 42.7

View. Looking north up the Fraser River we see the B.C. Railway bridge crossing the river. When the railway was built it was known as the Pacific Great Eastern of PGE: "Please Go Easy" to some of the locals. The railway allowed ranchers to transport cattle to Squamish and ship them from there to the market in Vancouver. In its early days the prospect of trains arriving on time was questionable. Apparently the best sign of an approaching train

The Bridge River rapids on the Fraser, just upstream of the Bridge River confluence, have a special reputation for treachery.

was the appearance of one conductor's "buckskin colored hound-dog, who would be coyote-trotting along the track ahead of the train a mile or so — his nose to the ground and stopping every so often to smell and sprinkle the stumps along the railroad track."

km 5.0/mi 3.1   **km 67.5**/mi 41.9
Side road. Some years ago this property was owned by Martin Chernault; it became a tourist attraction after he dug a 36-foot tunnel into the mountain and discovered a natural ice cave. Water dripping from the cave froze into icicles. There was little ice in the winter, but the hotter the weather became in summer, the more ice was formed. So many visitors came to see it that Chernault had to charge an admission fee to help pay for his time. This strange phenomenon came to an end in 1955 when B.C. Hydro began removing gravel from the hill to use in constructing the Seton Canal. Ice no longer formed in the cave.

km 5.7/mi 3.5   **km 66.8**/mi 41.5
The ponderosa pine and fir forest-stands alternate with more open areas of grassland and sage.

km 8.3/mi 5.1   **km 64.2**/mi 39.9
Cattleguard. Across the Fraser, the depleted waters of the Bridge River can be seen flowing into the Fraser. Waters that once flowed through the Bridge River Valley have been diverted into Seton Lake through two mountain tunnels, with the assistance of two dams, to produce power. Now only the few feeder streams below the Terzaghi Dam form the Bridge River.

The rapids on the Fraser River just upstream of the confluence are known as the Bridge River rapids and considered the most difficult on the Fraser. Commercial raft companies that take tours down the river every summer include Hell's Gate in their run, but usually must portage the Bridge River rapids. The Indians also considered this a rough piece of water and called the area "in-hoy-shtin" or "place of foam." On both sides of the river are old fishing shelters and drying racks — still used every year during the salmon runs, as they have been for many centuries.

On the wedge of land between the Bridge and Fraser is an abandoned Indian village. A few old cabins and the cemetery are all that are left of the community, the picturesque St. James Church having burned down in 1970.

km 10.5/mi 6.5   **km 62.0**/mi 38.5
Steep sparsely treed slopes can be seen across the Fraser, with the road zig-zagging up to service ranches further upstream. The road on the west side is the Watson Bar Road, described in Vol. 1,

Bridge River Country. It leads to the Poison Mountain area and the Big Bar Ferry.

km 14.3/mi 8.9   **km 58.2**/mi 36.1

Side road. A right turn heads south 28 kilometres through Fountain Valley and Three Lake Valley, which includes Kwotlenemo or Fountain Lake, Chilhil Lake and Cinquefoil Lake. The far end exits onto Highway 12. At one time there was a trading post called La Fontaine near the south end of the valley, and the route was sometimes used to bypass the "Big Slide" area on the trail between Lytton and Lillooet.

Although some sources indicate the name comes from a nearby natural spring or fountain, Bishop Hills (who came through here in 1860) says otherwise. It is "named for a Frenchman," he says, "intelligent, he speaks English well. He has been 27 years from home and has an aged mother who writes him long letters. He was born at Havre."

There are two BCFS recreation sites on this road. Kwotlenemo Lake North has good access for all vehicles, a boat launch and good fishing for Kamloops trout. Only electric motors may be used. It receives heavy use and is maintained summer and winter.

Kwotlenemo Lake South also has heavy use. It is a more open site with a marshy shoreline and another boat launch. It too is maintained summer and winter and is a good cross-country ski area. A map of the trails in the area is available from the Forest Service in Lillooet.

km 14.9/mi 9.2   **km 57.6**/mi 35.8

There are no formal picnic sites along this section of road; however, there is a little shade by a small creek here, where you can stop for a rest.

km 15.3/mi 9.5   **km 57.2**/mi 35.5

The road passes under a railway overpass of the B.C. Railway, the first of five crossings between here and Pavilion.

km 17.0/mi 10.6   **km 55.5**/mi 34.5

As the road continues upriver, a little whitewater can be seen below, one of the many nameless riffles that vary in size according to the season of the year and the height of water.

km 17.9/mi 11.1   **km 54.6**/mi 33.9

Gibbs Creek comes down from Chipuin Mountain in the Clear Range and crosses under the road to join the Fraser.

km 19.9/mi 12.3   **km 52.6**/mi 32.7

Here is one of the many Indian reserves left to the Indians along the Fraser, whose canyons and gorges have been home to native people for perhaps 9000 years. One site near Yale indicates continuous occupation for 5000 years. The ancestors of the Shuswap, Nl'akapxm and Stolo tribal nations lived on the benches left by prehistoric rivers and lakes fished for the salmon that ran up the river in the millions. Many of these reserves have since been cut up and isolated by the railways. Fishing trails were destroyed or blocked and fishing rocks covered by fill. The most severe damage was done when dumped rock waste caused the Hell's Gate slide of 1913. That slide wiped out nine of 10 salmon runs and left many upstream Indians without a winter food supply. Some of these runs have gradually been replaced by efforts of the International Pacific Salmon Fisheries Commission but they have still not reached their pre-slide numbers.

km 21.9/mi 13.6   **km 50.6**/mi 31.4
To the left of the road is Sallus Creek flowing west from Mt. Martley.

km 22.4/mi 13.9   **km 50.1**/mi 31.1
Rest stop.

km 23.4/mi 14.5   **km 49.1**/mi 30.5
15 Mile House. This important mile house was the first staging place after leaving Lillooet in the wagon road days. Dr. Cheadle and Lord Milton, two young Englishmen who toured the colony of British Columbia after walking from Canada across the prairies, passed this way in October of 1863. In his diary, Dr. Cheadle wrote a terse description of their first night out of Lillooet: "Stayed for night at 15-mile house; wretched place, no fire, no beds. Milton slept under the counter, I alongside it, Hall on the top; 4 or 5 miners along the floor." Accommodations were neither luxurious nor romantic.

km 24.1/mi 15.0   **km 48.4**/mi 30.1
Keatley Creek, another feeder creek, merges with the Fraser.

km 27.7/mi 17.2   **km 44.8**/mi 27.8
Irrigated fields and farms are along both sides of the Fraser.

km 28.8/mi 17.9   **km 43.7**/mi 27.1
Tiffin Creek flows down to the Fraser from the east. Just ahead a deep gorge on the far side of the river is where Slok Creek comes down from the west.

km 32.9/mi 20.4   **km 39.6**/mi 24.6
Pavilion general store. According to the *British Columbian*

newspaper of 1863, "the name [Pavilion] is French, taken from the flags there found floating over the Indian burial grounds by the Canadian Frenchmen, who first explored it."

The country store that stands here is the latest of several trading houses or stores that have serviced the Indians ranchers on both sides of the Fraser, and occasional tourists. My earliest recollection of the Pavilion store is of a neatly kept building with yellow roses growing by the porch; at that time simple meals were served in a homey atmosphere in a room to one side of the store. Though meals are no longer served, don't pass by without stopping for a cold drink or a browse around the friendly store.

km 34.2/mi 21.1   **km 38.3**/mi 23.8

A small Indian village with a neatly painted church is seen to the left, the Holy Trinity Roman Catholic Church. This is the site of the old 22 Mile House, where extra horses were stabled for the hard three-mile pull up Pavilion Mountain on the old wagon. The *British Columbian* referred to this as the Bridge Inn, and Dr. Cheadle called it Captain Martley's roadside house.

km 34.6/mi 21.5   **km 38.9**/mi 23.5

Junction. From this point Highway 12 continues along the Pavilion Valley by Pavilion Lake and Marble Canyon Park, through several Indian reserves, to Hat Creek House at Carquille, and the Trans-Canada Highway. In the early days there was an extensive farm up the Pavilion Valley called the Grange, "where with a soil derived from the 'disintegration of granite, metamorphic rocks, and crystalline limestone,' excellent crops of cereals and vegetables are produced." The Indians of the Pavilion area used to fight with other interior tribes in the Marble Canyon area and have left paintings or pictographs on the rocks in the canyon. They are marked by a sign.

According to one of the Pavilion Indian chiefs, whenever a chief died a painting on the rock would be done by his son. Figures and stars around such a figure indicated the chief's greatness. Another site about 5 km to the east of the marked pictographs has one of the finest panels of paintings in the Interior. The drawings are varied but include animals such as Bighorn sheep.

Before there were any roads through this area, the route to the Interior continued on a trail along the river. Even when the wagon road over Pavilion Mountain was built, the river trail was sometimes used as it was 35 miles shorter, though "much rougher and more hilly." It was a good day's walk to Leon, 10 miles from Pavilion. Leon was named for a Frenchman who ran a ferry service across the Fraser at a fare of 50 cents per passenger. He shafted passengers by representing the far side of the Fraser as a short and easy way, when in fact it was longer and more dangerous. The only advantage in crossing was a monetary one to Leon himself.

To follow the Cariboo Wagon Road, take a left turn and begin the steep tacking ascent of Pavilion Mountain.

km 38.8/mi 24.1   **km 33.7**/mi 20.9

To the southeast is Mount Cole, and farther east the Marble Mountains. One of three ranges between the Fraser Plateau and the Coast Mountains, the Marble Mountains are formed of limestone. Vegetation along the roadside now includes juniper, a creeping shrub with cedarlike branches and a pleasant aroma. It is a popular ornamental bush.

km 40.0/mi 24.8   **km 32.5**/mi 20.2

Topping a rise after climbing out of the Pavilion Valley, we find a large plateau and a picture-postcard view. Resting in a sea of grass flush with wild flowers, on a parklike hill dotted with clumps of aspen and pine, is the old Carson Ranch. Some people will know it as the old Spencer Ranch; now it is the Diamond S, with a sign requesting no trespassing except with written permission.

It had its beginning in 1858 when a young man by the name of Corson left Ohio on a wagon train bound for the Oregon coast. Disaster overtook the trekkers in the form of an Indian massacre. The doubtful story is that he was the only survivor. Robert Corson headed north following the fur brigade rail through the Okanagan and Kamloops to the Bonaparte Valley. He began packing supplies for miners and changed his name to Carson, since that was what everyone called him anyway. Wintering his animals on the grassy plateau of Pavilion Mountain he decided to stay there and farm. He built a cabin, barn and fences using logs from his own land, and brought limestone for his chimneys from Marble Canyon. He irrigated fields and began growing crops and hay.

Eventually Carson freighted his goods to the new Cariboo road at Clinton, and even drove cattle down the Harrison Trail to the coast and Gastown. There he met the woman who became his wife, returning with her to his kingdom above Marble Canyon. Gradually the house was enlarged to cope with a growing family, nine children in all.

Carson died in 1911 and his wife a few years later; both are buried on the ranch. One son, Robert, became the Provincial Minister of Public Works.

The ranch was operated by his son-in-law for years and then sold to Colonel Victor Spencer of Spencer stores. The Diamond S is now owned by J.E. Termuende of Vancouver.

km 43.3/mi 26.9   **km 29.2**/mi 18.1

Gillon Creek is crossed, one of the creeks draining Mount Carson, the peak to the southwest of Pavilion Mountain.

km 45.4/mi 28.2   **km 27.1**/mi 16.8

29 Mile House. On this bench, 29 Mile House was located. When we last came through, a few scattered ruins remained to mark the location of the second staging place from Lillooet, where extra teams were stabled for the final haul to the summit of Pavilion.

Wild flowers are beautiful here in early summer.

km 48.5/mi 30.1   **km 24.0**/mi 14.9

Side road. To the left an old forestry lookout road leads 1.2 kilometres to a ridge on the west. This may no longer be passable by car.

This point marks the summit of the Cariboo Road over Pavilion Mountain, about 1500 metres in elevation.

km 49.8/mi 30.9   **km 22.7**/mi 14.1

Side road. To the right is a road to the microwave tower and forestry lookout on the summit of Pavilion Mountain. Approximately 8 kilometres one way, this road would make a good hike in weather that is not too hot.

From here the road bridges Hambrook Creek and begins the descent down the famous Rattlesnake Grade. Though the road has improved, the description given by Butler and Cheadle of the road in 1863 obviously refers to the same hill: "We found ourselves on the brink of a precipitous descent of 2,000 feet, and in full view below saw the road following the configuration of the hill, with the numberless windings and zigzags which had given rise to its name. Everyone immediately volunteered to ease the poor horses by walking down, but Johny negatived the proposition at once, and drove us down at a furious rate, the heavily-laden wagon swinging around the sharp turns in a most unpleasant manner. The giving way of the break, or of a wheel, or the pole, must have been fatal; but all held together, as of course it was likely to do, and we reached the bottom safely."

km 53.3/mi 33.1   **km 19.2**/mi 11.9

Junction. Follow the road east on the north side of Kelly Lake.

km 54.9/mi 34.1   **km 17.7**/mi 11.0

Kelly Lake. This lake is named for Edward Kelly, a rancher who got his start near here in the 1860s. Some camping is available at the lake.

110

Widgeons nest in the reeds with other members of the duck family.

Downing Provincial Park at the east end of the lake is a small park but a fine place to stop for lunch or a night's rest. The land was donated by C.S. Downing.

km 56.3/mi 35.0   **km 16.2**/mi 10.1
Kelly Lake Junction. The road that cuts to the north here along Porcupine Creek is the Jesmond-Big Bar Road, detailed elsewhere in this volume. The ranch here is the Kelly Lake Ranch, established in 1866 by Edward Kelly.
Keep to the right to follow Cutoff Valley Creek through a beautiful glen about 16 kilometres to Clinton. From this point on, the route follows a two-lane gravel highway through mixed forest and long fields and private properties.

km 57.7/mi 35.8   **km 14.8**/mi 9.2
The road passes under a powerline which also follows along Cutoff Valley at Highway 97.

km 58.5/mi 36.3   **km 14.0**/mi 8.7
Kelly Lake B.C. Hydro substation.

km 60.1/mi 37.3   **km 12.4**/mi 7.7
B.C. Railway crossing.

km 62.0/mi 38.5   **km 10.5**/mi 6.5
A small lake to the right is about 1 kilometre long. Watch for ducks and waterfowl amongst the reeds, especially in springtime.

It is estimated that up to 80 per cent of the waterfowl in North America has its beginning (that is, hatches) in Canada. Often bluebirds are seen here on the fenceposts and flying over the fields, looking like cutouts against the azure summer sky. Also along the road are dusty wild roses, salsify, yarrow and asters.

km 68.0/mi 42.2   **km 4.5**/mi 2.8

Forty-two Creek has been passed, and pavement reached. Note the Russell fence on the right. The rows of timber supported by a tripod of posts made an economical fence to build on land with suitable trees and was often used when the ground was too hard for driving posts.

km 69.8/mi 43.3   **km 2.7**/mi 1.7

Spanish or Juan Ranch. The small square white building on the ranch to the right is where Cataline wintered his horses. Cataline, Jean Jacques Caux, was born in Oleron, Bearn, in what is now part of France and came to the Cariboo in the early 1860s. In partnership with Henry Castillou he started packing to the various gold camps. The Spanish or Juan Ranch, now the TR, was begun by one of Cataline's packers and served as a mule train relay station.

Cataline became known as the best packer in B.C., gaining a reputation as a drinker and for always wearing a boiled white shirt that was as clean at the end as at the beginning of each trip. When the Cariboo became too settled and crowded he moved to Hazelton and continued packing for many years. He took sick and died in 1922, and is buried in an unmarked grave overlooking Hazelton.

km 72.5/mi 45.0   **km 0**/mi 0

Clinton. This site was first an Indian village known as Sprague. When Tom Marshall and Joe Smith built the first hotel here in 1861 it was named 47 Mile House for its location on the original Cariboo wagon road. Then with the completion of the Cariboo Road through the canyon, it underwent another name change to become Clinton, after Henry Pelham Clinton, the Fifth Duke of Newcastle, Colonial Secretary in the British Government.

In the early days of the Cariboo Road, Clinton was the site of platform scales and a toll-gate, erected by contractor Gustavus Blin Wright, whose contract with the government allowed him to collect tolls for five to seven years in order to recoup some of his construction costs.

Now a major supply point for the surrounding area, the town has become the administrative centre of the Lillooet district. It has accommodations for tourists as well, but unfortunately the original Clinton Hotel built by Smith and Marshall is no longer there, having burned down in 1958 after almost a century of service. The Clinton Hotel was also the headquarters for the Annual Clinton Ball, a tradition that began in 1863 and continues in new quarters. The ball began to raise money for a library fund, with tickets selling for $10 per couple. Guests came from 200 miles around for a ball that was the social event of the year.

Clinton marks the final mileage on this route, which followed the old Cariboo Road from Lillooet to Clinton.

Seen from backroads as a tantalizing glimpse or a majestic vista, the Fraser River displays many moods. Here are two of them from the Big Bar area.

114

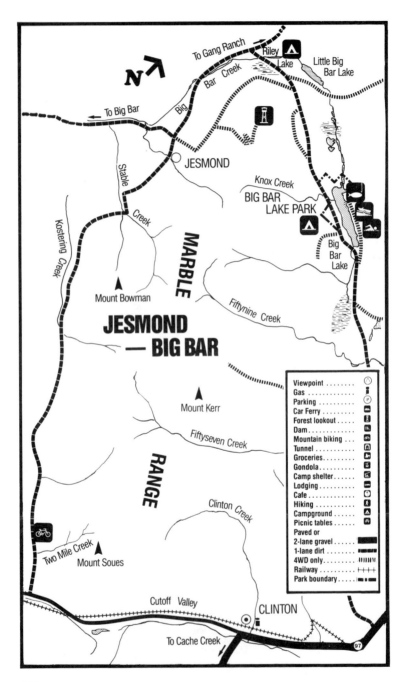

JESMOND
— BIG BAR

MARBLE

RANGE

To Gang Ranch

Riley Lake

Little Big Bar Lake

To Big Bar

Big Bar Creek

JESMOND

Stable Creek

Kostering Creek

Knox Creek

BIG BAR LAKE PARK

Big Bar Lake

Mount Bowman

Fiftynine Creek

Mount Kerr

Fiftyseven Creek

Clinton Creek

Two Mile Creek

Mount Soues

Cutoff Valley

CLINTON

To Cache Creek

97

N

Viewpoint . . . .
Gas . . . .
Parking . . . .
Car Ferry . . . .
Forest lookout . . . . .
Dam . . . .
Mountain biking . . .
Tunnel . . . .
Groceries . . . .
Gondola . . . .
Camp shelter . . . . . .
Lodging . . . .
Cafe . . . .
Hiking . . . .
Campground . . . . . .
Picnic tables . . . . . .
Paved or
2-lane gravel . . . . . .
1-lane dirt . . . .
4WD only . . . .
Railway . . . .
Park boundary . . . . .

116

Route Eight

Jesmond and Big Bar

The Marble Mountains are one of three small ranges between the Coast Mountains and the Fraser Plateau. The grey-white limestone ridges of the Marble Range, formed by a long process of deposit, compression and uplift, mark the watershed line between the Fraser and Thompson Rivers from Pavilion Creek north to Big Bar Creek. Around the perimeter of the northern half of this range, the Jesmond-Big Bar road loops from Kelly Lake junction on the old Cariboo Road north of Clinton. A complete circle may be made by continuing to Clinton and then along the section of the old Cariboo Road that runs through Cutoff Valley.

Set against the majestic marble backdrop are forested slopes that support fast-running streams, homesteads, guest ranches and small logging operations; and open meadows with a wealth of lakes, potholes and swamps, typical of cattle country. Recreation opportunities of the area include boating, canoeing, fishing, horseback riding, hiking, hunting and bird watching. There is also a campground and picnic site at Big Bar Lake.

The Jesmond-Big Bar road and its tributary roadways provide access as well to the Chilcotin country and the Fraser River, to a forestry lookout in the Marble Mountains, and to the attractive expanse of Big Bar Mountain. Place names like Kostering Creek, Beaverdam Lake and the Devil's Garden honor some of the pioneer ranchers of the area and reflect the history and natural history of the country.

The main route to Jesmond and Big Bar Lake is a good gravel road that would pose no problem to the average vehicle. Side roads are not all-weather roads, and should be avoided when the weather is wet or when muddy from melting snow; the gumbo that forms is tricky to drive through and messy to get bogged down in.

Maps

National Topographic Series 1:50,000 92 P/4 W Clinton; 92 P/5 W Jesmond; 92 P/5 E Jesmond; 92 P/4 E Clinton or B.C. Lands and Forests Series 1:125,000 92 P Bonaparte River.

km 0/mi 0   **km 90.5**/mi 56.2

Begin this route 16 kilometres west of Clinton along the old Cariboo Road at the Kelly Lake junction. Turn north at the road signed to Kelly Lake, Canoe Creek Road and Jesmond on a well-maintained, two-lane gravel road. Hints of the old west linger in the warning sign that the area is patrolled by Clinton and District Range Patrol; rustling is still a problem and the cattlemen have banded together to control it.

km 0.7/mi 0.4   **km 89.8**/mi 55.8

Management Unit 3-31 of the British Columbia Fish and Wildlife Branch begins here; Kelly Creek and Cutoff Valley Creek form the border between it and unit 3-17. These administrative boundaries were set up in 1975, dividing the province into seven regions with 216 management units to aid in resource management and define hunting area. The efforts of Fish and Wildlife to do a more effective job of management have unfortunately resulted in a proliferation of signs marking the units along highways, byways and backroads throughout the province.

The road passes several private properties, through mixed forest or fir, pine, spruce, juniper, trembling aspen and cottonwood. Scattered along the roadside are patches of wild flowers in rainbow shades — yellow mullein, dandelions, salsify and stonecrop; orange tiger lilies; orange-red Indian paintbrush; mauve-pink clover, vetches, penstemon, thistle, asters and fireweed; blue lupines; and creamy yarrow.

km 5.4/mi 3.3   **km 85.1**/mi 52.8

Side road. A log hauling road goes off up to the right through the trees.

km 10.5/mi 6.5   **km 80.0**/mi 49.7

The road follows Porcupine Creek, which can be seen to the left among the willows. A hydro line clings to the right side of the road.

km 11.5/mi 7.1   **km 79.0**/mi 49.1

Side road. To the left a side road climbs onto a ridge of the Edge Hills and then switchbacks steeply down to High Bar on the Fraser

There's a special magic in an early-morning visit to Big Bar Lake.

River. Reports say that the road does go through; both times that we tried it, though, we were unable to negotiate the mud. At the Fraser is the High Bar Indian Reserve and a road heading north from High Bar to exit on the side road running between Jesmond and Big Bar Ferry.

km 12.4/mi 7.7   **km 78.1**/mi 48.5
The Marble Mountain Range can be seen ahead, rising to 2100 metres.

km 12.8/mi 7.9   **km 77.7**/mi 48.2
The first of a couple of marshy ponds lies here, surrounded by grasses. In spring and early summer, such ponds are good places to watch for ducks — mallards or others nesting or with their young — and for spotted sandpipers bobbing and dashing about. Almost hidden in the grass are dainty blue forget-me-nots. There is a corral here too. Watch for livestock as you continue down the road.

km 14.5/mi 9.0   **km 76.0**/mi 47.2
A small creek crosses under the road.

km 15.2/mi 9.4   **km 75.3**/mi 46.8
The powerline meets the road and continues on the right-hand side.

km 15.5/mi 9.6   **km 75.0**/mi 46.6
Cattleguard. A sign at Limestone Mountain Ranch welcomes

visitors. Horses grazing in the fields nearby are a reminder that this is good riding country. Beyond the ranch is a beaver lodge and a swamp.

km 16.1/mi 10.1   **km 74.4**/mi 46.2

The road cuts through an esker at this point. It's a sign that glaciers once passed this way, as an esker is a ridge of gravel deposited by a glacial stream from a retreating glacier. Between 10 and 20,000 years ago, most of British Columbia was under one to two miles of ice, spreading from seed glaciers still present in the Rocky Mountains, Though no one really knows why an ice age begins, all that seems necessary is a decrease of five degrees Celsius in the annual average temperature so that more ice builds up every winter than melts in the summer. The difference in temperature may be caused by fluctuations in the sun's energy. Much of the province's landscape bears marks of the last glaciation.

km 16.4/mi 10.2   **km 74.1**/mi 46.0

The road passes a small ranch as it meets up with Kostering Creek and then begins to follow it north for a short distance through an area decorated with Indian paintbrush, tiger lilies and soopolallie.

According to Harry Marriott in his book *Cariboo Cowboy,* the Kosterings were a pioneer family who had a good place on the banks of the Fraser, at the mouth of Big Bar Creek. They used Big Bar Creek to irrigate crops. Kostering Creek is a feeder creek of Big Bar; there is a Mount Kostering at the north end of the Edge Hills.

km 19.1/mi 11.9   **km 71.4**/mi 44.3

Edge Hills to the left separate this valley from the Fraser River. The meadow on the left is enclosed in a snake fence. Though it uses a lot of material and energy to build, it is very strong. Another advantage is that a panel is easily removed to drive stock through.

The leaves of the soopolallie are silvery-green and have rusty-looking markings on their undersides as well as on the branches. The almost transparent red berries grow on bushes about a metre in height; they were collected by the Indians by shaking a branch over a basket. Though they have an extremely bitter taste, they were considered a great treat by the Indians, who were not accustomed to artificially sweetened foods. Beaten up with sugar, the unusual "soap berry" loses some of its bitterness and even a non-native can acquire a taste for it.

km 21.7/mi 13.5   **km 68.8**/mi 42.7

A small creek crosses under the road, a side stream of Kostering Creek running down between Mount Deer and Mount Bowman. Mount Kerr probably honors another of the early ranching families in the area, as Ike Kerr had a ranch near Big Bar Lake.

km 22.4/mi 13.9   **km 68.1**/mi 42.3

Circle H Guest Ranch. This ranch offers cabins, trail rides, meals in the ranchhouse and cross-country skiing.

km 26.1/mi 16.2   **km 64.4**/mi 40.0

Buckets of paintbrush give the ground cover a red tone and brighten the landscape during the height of the blooming season. The tiny flowers of this colorful plant are green; the bracts are brilliantly decked in crimson, red, orange, yellow or white. It is the red or orange, though, that is most familiar.

km 27.9/mi 17.3   **km 62.6**/mi 38.9

Side road. A side road goes off to the left, the first of three over the next couple of kilometres. At least two of these appear to be logging roads.

km 30.2/mi 18.7   **km 60.3**/mi 37.4

The road passes under a powerline.

km 30.8/mi 19.1   **km 59.7**/mi 37.1

Circle C Ranch.

km 31.0/mi 19.2   **km 59.5**/mi 36.9

A small loop goes off to the left.

km 31.4/mi 19.5   **km 59.1**/mi 36.7

Cattleguard, and powerline again. We pass Stable Creek homestead.

km 32.9/mi 20.4   **km 57.6**/mi 35.8

Side road. The powerline cuts are almost the only places along the road here to pull off for a lunch stop or to stretch the legs a little. To the left under the powerline is an ideal spot since it offers a view to the west of the meadows on Big Bar Mountain. You sit surrounded by a great variety of small wild flowers, including the white flowered northern bedstraw, with a squarish stem you can feel by twirling it between your fingers; nodding onion, with a pale mauve flower; and wild strawberry, white petalled or (better still) with tiny sweet red berries almost hidden under the leaves.

Cattle have grazed on Big Bar Mountain, named for a bar on the Fraser River, for many years. The Big Bar range was one of many pastures used by Gang Ranch until new settlers began to move in, building homes and fences and gradually pushing the cattle back into more timbered areas. By 1941, there were about a dozen homesteads on Big Bar Mountain. Most of the settlers had just enough food and tools to get started; their small parcels of land, called dry farms, had too little precipitation and were later plagued with grasshoppers. Gradually the settlers gave up and left, and after many years the ploughed land returned to grass.

km 35.2/mi 21.9　　　　　　　　　　**km 55.2**/mi 34.3

A side road to the right is followed by a side road to the left, signed "Grinder." This is the name of another pioneer family of the area. Phil Grinder was a Pennsylvania Dutchman who came to the area in the 1860s looking for gold. He settled at Big Bar and married and raised a family; several of his descendants also lived and ranched in the same area. He was well known for his practical jokes. According to his friend Harry Marriott, once when the two of them were looking at a steep slope, Phil remarked, "Harry, if you are ever riding your saddle horse coming down those trails off the mountains, be sure and keep your shirt collar snugged up around your neck — riding downhill is so steep that a horse might drop a hot bun right down your back."

Life was not easy in the early days, but it must have been a healthy existence. Old Phil stuck around until he was in his mid-nineties, succumbing to pneumonia in December 1914.

km 36.6/mi 22.5　　　　　　　　　　**km 53.9**/mi 33.7

Jesmond. The log house and barn, fields, and wild roses growing along the fence make Jesmond as lovely a spot as the name suggests. Earlier known as "Mountain House," this ranch was run for many years by the Coldwell family and functioned as a post office and sometimes a store for the Big Bar area. During the days of the weekly mail stage, the mail would arrive at Jesmond every Wednesday evening. Horses and drivers would be put up overnight at the Coldwell place before heading to Dog Creek and Alkali Lake the next day.

km 37.6/mi 23.3　　　　　　　　　　**km 52.9**/mi 32.8

Junction. The road passes under the powerline as the junction to Big Bar ferry is reached. A left turn on a road through the narrow valley of Big Bar Creek leads 19 kilometres to a reaction ferry crossing of the Fraser River. En route several ranches are passed, and another road turns south along the Fraser to High Bar.

Homesteads along the Big Bar route couldn't always make a go of it.

The ferryman lives in a house just above the ferry landing. Free crossings are available on request during the following hours: 7 a.m. to noon; 1 p.m. to 5 p.m.; and 6 p.m. to 7 p.m. The toll for emergency crossings outside regular hours is $5. Though the ferry does not operate during the winter due to ice, usually from about December to April, foot passengers can be taken across by cable car.

Route options available on the west side of the Fraser from Big Bar include Watson Bar Creek road and the Yalakom road. However, both these present some difficulties and are not always passable. They should not be attempted without some knowledge of the area as well as good maps, adequate backroading equipment, extra gas, extra food, and preferably a second vehicle. Often the Big Bar ferryman will be the best current source of information on whether vehicles are making it through either route. Both the Yalakom and Watson Bar routes are detailed in Vol. 1 of this series.

Keep right at the **km 37.6** junction to continue on the main Jesmond-Big Bar route.

km 37.8/mi 23.5   **km 52.7**/mi 32.7

Side road. A right turn under the powerline leads to a side road that climbs up the Marble Range to Jesmond Lookout, which provides hikers or backroaders with vehicles capable of a steep climb with a marvellous aerial view of the southern Cariboo country. This one-lane road is definitely a dry-weather road, as it

High above the Fraser Canyon, at an elevation of almost 6500 feet, the Jesmond Lookout offers a spectacular view.

becomes very muddy when wet. Take right turns at km 1.8 and km 3.9 along the side road; a sign "Jesmond Lookout" lets you know you're on the right track.

The lower part of the Jesmond Lookout road passes through a large logged-off clearing and an old mill site, then continues through second-growth forest, lined with many shrubs and wild flowers. As the sidehills are crossed the landscape becomes more parklike, with grassy slopes underlying the tall timber, more wild flowers, and a chipmunk or two. The view to the west is out over Big Bar Mountain. Soon the alpine meadows are reached, crowded with a great assortment of small flowers. Western anemones, field chickweed, stonecrop, vetches, penstemon, asters and yarrow are added to the list of flowers seen lower on the road such as wild rose, fireweed, Indian paintbrush, wild strawberries, goldenrod, northern bedstraw, wild flax, brown-eyed susans, dandelions and salsify.

The road begins to ascend, gradually at first, then steeply across side hills and around hairpin bends. At km 9.3 there is a widening of the road suitable for parking; we recommend that you *do* park — unless you are driving a 4x4 — since the road climbs at about a 15-degree angle through loose gravel and large rocks. Also, from this point it is a fairly short walk to reach the top, and walking gives a better opportunity to enjoy the alpine flowers and absorb the view.

Finally the top of the incline is reached and we see the forest lookout tower — a reminder of a solitary spartan existence, with the necessities of life and a small garden — wild flowers and a great view. Elevation at the lookout is 6464 feet. Landmarks can be identified with the help of a map: Mount Kostering, Fraser Canyon, Camelsfoot Range across the Fraser, Big Bar Mountain, China Lake, Chilcotin road, Meadow Lake, Big Bar Lake, Little White Lake, Green Lake and the ridges of the Marble Mountains.

An alternate route back from the lookout is to turn right or north at the km 3.9 junction and continue around the shoulder of the Marble Range to rejoin the main road near Big Bar Lake at **km 50.9.**

Back at the main road keep left to continue the route.

km 38.2/mi 23.7   **km 52.3**/mi 32.5
Echo Springs Ranch.

km 40.0/mi 24.8   **km 50.5**/mi 31.4
Cattleguard. A side track goes off to the right.

km 41.2/mi 25.6   **km 49.3**/mi 30.6
Big Bar Creek crossing. The road continues past a large swamp area, by a lake, and through a grassy meadow. Killdeer plovers can often be seen in the area in the early summer. Watch for broken-wing acts by these birds, an indication that a nest or young birds are nearby. The nests are usually so well camouflaged, spotted blotchy beige eggs in a small depression in gravel, that they are extremely difficult to see. The handsome adult birds have a distinctive call when disturbed, sounding like "kill deer," for which they are named.

To the east, Marble Mountain Lookout can be seen.

km 42.2/mi 26.2   **km 48.3**/mi 30.0
To the right a road leads to a log house. This luxurious home was built and owned by George Harrison, who lived in Vancouver but visited the OK Ranch frequently in his capacity as a partner in the ranch and manager of the business end. It is now privately owned.

Yellow-bellied marmots make their home in rocky areas by the meadow on the right. These rodents belong to the same family as squirrels and chipmunks but are larger, with stout bodies and short bushy tails. They are chestnut colored, with pale buff or yellowish markings on the sides of the neck and under the abdomen. Other distinguishing marks include white spots on the face in front of the eyes. This area is typical of where they live, in the southern, hotter areas of the province in grassland, near treed areas. They feed on plant materials and hibernate for a long stretch over the winter.

Yellow-bellied marmots are often hosts to a tick that causes paralysis in man and domestic animals. Rocky Mountain or paralysis wood ticks are prevalent in the spring and early summer in the dry grassland areas of British Columbia. They depend on blood for existence and attach themselves to passing mammals, including man. To feed, the female tick attaches her mouth parts to the host by producing a quick-drying cement.

Symptoms of paralysis develop only after the tick has been feeding for about five days; they begin with a numbness and gradual paralysis of the lower limbs, progressing to hands and arms and eventually to the throat muscles. This will result in death unless the tick is removed. If it is removed in time, however, complete recovery from the paralysis follows. To avoid tick paralysis a daily examination of the body should be made when you are in tick country between April and June; pay special attention to hairline areas. To remove ticks, use tweezers and apply a slow, gentle pull.

Just beyond the road to the log house, the main road crosses a creek. There is a box canyon off to the left, and a short walk leads to an old dam. A Pelton water wheel and pumphouse provided electric power to OK Ranch for many years.

km 42.7/mi 26.5   **km 47.8**/mi 29.7

OK Ranch Buildings. The weathered green buildings, now abandoned, are testimony to busier, active days. This property was originally known as the old Haller homestead, part of a 3000-acre spread owned by Joe Haller, a Bavarian who emigrated to the colony of British Columbia in 1859. For over 40 years the Hallers, Grinders and Kosterings, with their descendants, were the main inhabitants of the Big Bar area, living off ranching supplemented with odd jobs on roads or other ranches, growing their own gardens, hunting deer and catching salmon.

In 1933 the old Haller place and several other properties owned by Harry Marriott were consolidated by Marriott into the OK Ranch Company Limited in partnership with George Harrison of Vancouver. For 17 years Marriott managed the OK Ranch with the assistance of his wife and son and Harrison's advice and support. Their many enterprises included beef, pork and turkeys. In 1950 OK Ranch was sold to a U.S. businessman.

km 43.0/mi 26.7   **km 47.5**/mi 29.5

Side road. The road to the left leads to the grassy meadows with island of pine and fir forest on Big Bar Mountain. Though topographical maps show roads circling the mountain and joining the Jesmond road at **km 46.0,** our experience proved that the road no longer goes through. However, it is still an interesting area to explore. The road branches several times. If we keep right at every junction, the road winds across large open meadows where cows graze, past potholes used by ducks, and into a logging area. Back at km 2.5, on the Big Bar side road, take a left turn past Poison Lake, continue right at km 6.4 (a left at this point goes along Kashburn Road to a plateau overlooking the Fraser River above French Bar Canyon) and then meander around the south side of Big Bar Mountain.

The dry-weather road passes through areas of wild flowers, trees and logging areas. The scenery includes an old cabin and such birds as killdeer, meadow larks, marsh hawks, flickers, bluebirds and grouse. The turnaround point for us was when we were confronted with a two-metre hole dug across the road at about the 1150-metre level at Deadman Creek. It would be about four kilometres farther to Crows Bar Creek.

km 43.2/mi 26.8   **km 47.3**/mi 29.4

A view across the valley reveals the large Harrison log house and pool. The road continues past several potholes and lakes, excellent places to find waterfowl.

km 45.6/mi 28.3   **km 44.9**/mi 27.9

Cattleguard.

km 46.0/mi 28.6   **km 44.5**/mi 27.6

Side road. A side track back to the left is the road to Devil's Garden and around the north side of Big Bar Mountain. The wide rough track passes through pine forest and grass 4.7 kilometres to a meadow overlooking China Lake. Scattered through the grass are sage, juniper, foxtail varley, salsify, yarrow, thistle and rocks seemingly whitewashed by the sun. The area north of China Lake is Devil's Garden, where glacial erratics and volcanic bombs are strewn over the ground in an eerie manner.

Though somewhat rutty and muddy, the road continues on past munching cows, nesting birds, potholes, an old mill site and a marshy area, and comes to a stop at a fence labelled "No trespassing" just beyond an aspen grove. Roads continue beyond the fence and beyond the mill site, but with the one fenced and the other very obscure and cluttered with debris, they are not passable. It would be interesting to hike from the mill site around to meet the **km 43.0** road to Deadman Creek, or down to the Fraser through China Gulch where rock formations are unusual and inspiring.

James Teit recorded an Indian legend about the riverside sculptures: "Once in ancient times, the Crees from the east, the Thompsons from the south, and the Lillooet from the west made up their minds to attack and there joined forces. Numbering several hundred men, they now advanced up the river to attack Shuswap, but when nearly opposite the mouth of Lone Cabin Creek and still some distance from Canoe Creek, they were met by Coyote, or some other transformer, who changed them into pillars of clay. They may be seen standing there now — the tall Crees on the right, the Thompson of medium height in the centre, and the short Lillooet on the left."

km 46.5/mi 28.9   **km 44.0**/mi 27.3

Junction. The road to the left goes to Canoe Creek and through to the Chilcotin. It was this road and the junction to the right that formed the early trail and road used by Gang Ranch and other ranches in the area to commute to Clinton on the Cariboo Road for supplies. Churn Creek ferry, formerly used to cross the Fraser at Gang Ranch, was replaced by a bridge in 1912. According to the ferryman, Bill Wright, anyone who drank water from the Fraser River there would always come back to it again sooner or later. The water was muddy in those days, but definitely not as polluted as it is now.

Keep right at this junction to continue the route past Big Bar Lake.

km 47.0/mi 29.2   **km 43.5**/mi 27.0

The road passes under a powerline, then alongside a swamp to the right. There are some primitive camping areas on the left.

km 47.4/mi 29.4   **km 43.1**/mi 26.8

Riley Dam Recreation Site is located here on Big Bar Creek. Cutting between Riley Lake and another smaller lake, the road crosses a cattleguard and passes through heavier pine forest.

km 48.4/mi 30.1   **km 42.1**/mi 26.1

Side track to right.

km 49.7/mi 30.9   **km 40.8**/mi 25.3

Side road to the left leads to Little Big Bar Lake and a BCFS recreation site. The lake offers fishing and interesting canoeing.

km 50.9/mi 31.6   **km 39.6**/mi 24.6

The side road to the right goes south to link up with the side road to Jesmond Lookout at **km 37.8.**

km 51.5/mi 32.3   **km 38.4**/mi 23.8

Side track to the right. Yarrow and Northern bedstraw underlie the pine and trembling aspen along the route. It rejoins the main road at km 54.2.

km 55.5/mi 34.5   **km 35.0**/mi 21.7
Side track to the right.

km 56.9/mi 35.3   **km 33.6**/mi 20.9
Side track to right. This is another of the old logging areas; the road fans out but deteriorates within two to three kilometres after passing two mill sites. Four-wheel drives could take most of the roads a little farther, but headway seems to peter out before long. Coyote droppings and moose droppings on the road suggest that those mammals may be seen in the area.

km 58.3/mi 36.2   **km 32.2**/mi 20.0
Big Bar Lake Provincial Campground. Beautifully situated on the west end of this grassland lake is a campsite, picnic site and boat launch. The lake is popular for Kamloops trout and for canoeing. At the far end of the lake is a march and beaver lodge and on the lake in early summer you are likely to see loons and golden-eyes with young. Yellow butterflies float through the air; dragonflies and damselflies hover near the water.

Around the campground watch for chipmunks and squirrels, muledeer and bear (or for signs of them, like tracks, dung or marking on trees). Many of the common wild flowers are around, and some seen less often such as strawberry blight, pyrola, star-flowered Solomon's seal, cinquefoil, and water parsnip. The twilight and early morning hours are the only times when mosquitos become a nuisance, breeding in large numbers in the many potholes and swamps nearby; they quickly disappear in the heat of the day.

km 59.2/mi 36.8   **km 31.3**/mi 19.4
Cattleguard.

km 62.7/mi 38.6   **km 27.8**/mi 17.3
View. From the side hill to the left, we can see the eastern end of Big Bar Lake and large grassy glades interrupting forested areas.

km 63.3/mi 39.3   **km 27.2**/mi 16.9
Marriott Road. The side road to the left follows around the eastern end of Big Bar Lake to the flat on the northeast side of the lake that was chosen as a homestead site by Harry Marriott in 1919. He and his wife Peg moved into their cabin by the lake in the winter of 1923, and added a barn and corral to their holdings. There were other moves for them and their son Ronnie, but they kept the Big Bar property. In 1931 they returned to it to begin a new venture, a guest ranch and fishing camp. Over the years, it was built into a very successful business, with cabins, boats, horses

and homemade meals. It was Peg Marriott's special project, and eventually she owned and managed it. Now she has retired, but the Big Bar Guest Ranch and Fishing Camp is still there, having added many camp spots along the lake for the benefit of guests.

Just beyond the Marriott Road turnoff is a cattleguard. To the right is a beaver pond with the Marble Mountain Range in the background.

km 66.6/mi 41.5   **km 23.9**/mi 14.8

Side road. After passing a marshy area, a side track cuts back to the left. Though there is really nothing spectacular along this side road to Beaverdam Lake, it is pleasant to wander across the grassy meadows and alongside lakes and marshes, observing the birdlife and plants. First the track skirts around a couple of arms of the strangely shaped little White Lake, then by Fiftynine Creek and Beaverdam Lake to join with the main road running between the Cariboo Highway and the Chilcotin. The length of this side track is 11 kilometres.

Birders will be able to identify many species, but almost anyone passing this way will recognize bluebirds, blackbirds, sandpipers, flickers and horned larks. In early summer the fields become gardens of wild flowers: brow-eyed susans, Indian paintbrush, stonecrop, yarrow, vetches, asters and erigonium. Other things to watch include a study plot, about halfway along the route, and a Russell fence near the Chilcotin Road. At the junction with the Chilcotin Road, a left turn goes past Meadow Lake to Canoe Creek and Dog Creek. To the right is the Cariboo Highway.

km 70.8/mi 44.0   **km 19.7**/mi 12.2

Back on the Big Bar Road, the route continues to be lined with wild flowers. A creek crosses under the road, a cattleguard cuts the road, and we notice a snake fence that has been given more support by extra posts.

km 73.1/mi 45.4   **km 17.4**/mi 10.8

Cattleguard and homestead.

km 73.3/mi 45.8   **km 16.8**/mi 10.4

Pothole.

km 76.1/mi 47.2   **km 14.4**/mi 8.9

Side road. To the right a road turns off and then circles around to Fiftyseven Creek. The route now is through pine and fir forests.

km 82.9/mi 51.5   **km 7.6**/mi 4.7

Ranch at Fiftyseven Creek.

If you're lucky — or a good planner — your travels will take you to a rodeo where you can enjoy the bull-riding.

km 83.9/mi 52.1   **km 6.6**/mi 4.1
Powerline.

km 86.7/mi 53.8   **km 3.8**/mi 2.3
Side road to right.

km 87.0/mi 54.6   **km 2.6**/mi 1.6
Side road to right.

km 88.8/mi 55.1   **km 1.7**/mi 1.1
Landing strip, after which a side road to the right is passed.

km 90.1/mi 55.9   **km 0.4**/mi 0.2
The road descends to the highway.

km 90.5/mi 56.2   **km 0**/mi 0
Cariboo Highway. The route description of the Jesmond Big Bar Route ends here. Clinton is about 10 kilometres to the south along the Cariboo Highway. For those who are hooked on backroading, there are many more roads to discover and explore in this area. All you need is a little time and curiosity (as well as gas and maps) for many rewarding hours, days or weekends.

Appendix A
Forest Road Travel

The Ministry of Forests' *Guide for Safe Travel* recommends a number of precautions for travel on roads used by industrial logging traffic. These roads lead to areas that would otherwise be difficult of access, but there are potential dangers.

First, check with the local Forest Service office before using any road. It will be able to provide some maps and local advice.

In transit, yield to oncoming industrial traffic. As any experienced backroader knows, logging trucks use all or most of the road — whether they need it not — and travel faster than other traffic. Logging traffic always has the right-of-way and "right-of-weight." When you see logging traffic, find a turn-out and get off the road. Forest Service reminds you that whichever side a turn-out is on "it is your responsibility to get to it."

Stay alert and ready to take evasive action. Drive defensively. Obey all speed limits and road signs. Drive with your lights on. Do not block the road to take a photo or admire the view. Pull well off the travelled portion of the road.

Do not haul travel-trailers on logging roads. Loaded trucks will not be able to back up steep grades. This may leave you having to back your rig and trailer down a winding road for several hundred metres.

Signs often indicate a radio-controlled road. This does not mean a Citizen's Band (CB) radio. If your two-way radio can pick up logging company frequencies be sure it is working. Following a radio-controlled logging rig is always the best advice.

Sweepers, extra-long logs up to 70 feet, are sometimes loaded on logging trucks. They are too long to be hauled on public roads and can hang over the back of trailers by 20 feet. On tight corners they

A CB radio provides reliable two-way communication for anyone venturing into the back country.

can literally sweep a car off the edge. You may be asked to drive on the left side for this reason. Be careful of sweepers even if you see a parked truck. There may be a corner ahead hiding a sweeper.

Roads are not as well maintained as public highways so keep an eye out for road damage including washouts, potholes, slides and flooding.

To report fires, vandalism or road damage, dial '0' and ask for Zenith 5555.

Appendix B
Backroading Equipment

Turning your vehicle off a well-travelled paved road onto a gravel or dirt byway can be the start of an exciting and pleasurable adventure. For those who are unprepared, however, and who don't take certain precautions, it can be the start of a very unpleasant adventure, and in some cases even cause injury or death. The key phrase for all backroading is — *be prepared*.

Obviously the state of preparedness is going to depend on the length of your backroad trip and the condition of the road. With this in mind we can look at two types of backroader and two lists of emergency equipment. One type would be the casual backroader who expects nothing worse than a gravel road with perhaps the odd muddy section. The other would be someone expecting all kinds of road conditions from fallen trees to creek fords. Consider, though, that either set of problems could be faced by even the most casual of backroaders. A heavy rain or early snowfall can quickly change road conditions. Once again, be prepared.

Essential equipment

Everyone using this book should be carrying the following equipment:
- A good spare tire, or two
- A working jack, preferably with a large base
- A few 2x4s for a jacking base
- A shovel or entrenching tool
- A sharp axe
- Tire chains for mud or snow
- A tow rope or chain
- Extra gas
- Extra water
- Flashlight
- First-aid kit.

Extra equipment

To the above list a serious backroader — for instance, someone trying the Hurley Pass, Yalakom or Watson Bar Road — should add the following:

- A second large jack
- A full size shovel
- A come-a-long or block-and-tackle set
- A steel bar or pick
- A tool kit including spare nuts, bolts, a spring and bailing wire
- Radiator sealant
- A saw, such as a Swede saw or small chain saw
- Signal aids, large flashlight, flares and mirror
- Spare belts for the engine
- A fire extinguisher
- A tire pump or air transfer tube
- A large wheel wrench
- Extra cable for the winch
- Jumper cables
- Clothes and boots suitable for walking out
- Sleeping bags or blankets
- Tire repair kit and tools
- Extra food and water
- Still more gas
- A water bucket, folding type.

You may also consider including spare parts like a fuel pump, water pump, spark plugs, points, radiator hoses, high pressure hoses, and other parts, tools or aids (such as a service manual) that may be important or peculiar to your rig or driving style. Parts can be important not only if you do your own repair work but also if you break down in a remote town where parts have to be shipped in.

Being prepared is certainly the most important thing in backroading; road precautions are a close second, for if you don't take some you can be sure you will need all the equipment and more. A few classic situations should be checked out thoroughly:

- If you are driving a heavy rig be sure to check out all bridges. Some you will find no longer in use, and a ford will be nearby. You get only one chance on these spots.

- Mudholes should be checked for depth, and to see if they have a firm bottom and give enough clearance for your vehicle. (Do you know your rig's clearance and where the low points are?)
- Don't go down a hill you may not be able to get back up. Be sure the road is passable beyond before proceeding. And conversely don't go up a steep hill without checking it out. You may find that you have to back down through slippery sections where you could lose your brakes.
- Fords and creek crossings should be attempted only by experienced drivers. Check the depth and bottom, and the angle of descent and ascent from the creek. Will your vehicle's bottom drag? Once out, be sure to dry off your brakes before proceeding.
- Slides and rolling rocks should be levelled and moved before proceeding. (After you have tipped, or a rock has torn out your oil pan or gas tank, it is too late.) Traditionally this has been the passenger's job and on rough roads it can be excellent exercise. Sometimes you will wish you had a shovel for each person — a possibility to consider on a road where slides are expected.

You will, of course, be taking the equipment and precautions in the hope that you are not going to need any of them. It is likely though that you will use at least some. Let's suppose for a moment that you do have vehicle trouble or get stuck; perhaps the road washes out or a heavy snow fall traps you. A number of things can be done to keep your vehicle moving, ease it out, or make your stay more comfortable:

- A damaged radiator can be plugged in an emergency with rags, wood or a bar of soap. Porridge or other expanding wheat cereals added to radiator coolant will plug the hole from the inside; of course, you could use the can of radiator sealant that you brought.
- Leaky hoses can be repaired with tape or string in some cases. Removing the rad cap will lower the pressure, but keep your revs low.
- A punctured gas tank can be sealed with chewing gum, a bar of soap, "seal-all" or a product called stove cement, designed for cementing stove parts and fire-pots.
- A broken brakeline can be crimped between the leak and the hydraulic pump. This means one or more brakes will not be functioning. Spare brake fluid will help.
- Vapor lock can occur in overheated engines when you are travelling slowly or climbing. Usually it is caused by overheated fuel lines near the engine. Symptoms are the same as running out of fuel. Cool all lines, carburetor and fuel pump with wet rags. If the carb is flooded hold the accelerator to the floor and turn the

engine over. Do not pump the pedal.

• If you are running low on gas, decrease your speed, keep your revs constant and coast wherever possible.

What to do when stuck

Losing traction in mud, snow or sand (getting stuck) is often caused by improper weight distribution. The first thing to try is adding weight to the drive wheels. Have passengers stand on the back or add rocks or sand. Sometimes just a push will get you over the slippery section. After that, try using floor mats, branches or sand to add traction. If you are really bogged down you may have to jack up your vehicle and gradually build a road out. Drain away any water first of all, then give the mud some time to dry a little.

A spare tire, table top, 2x4s, or even luggage can be used as an emergency base for a jack. Lighten your load by removing all heavy items and draining the holding tank or water supply. If you don't have a winch or come-a-long to pull yourself out, try using a large jack as a winch.

Tall jacks can also be used to jack the vehicle up and then push it sideways. We once actually turned a small pickup around in the middle of a mudhole by this method. However, it has been known to break axles.

If you are badly stuck, take your time. Trying to hurry out of a bad spot often results in getting in deeper. Figure on spending an hour or two and make the proper preparations before trying to drive out.

If you are stuck fast, or your vehicle is broken down to the extent that you have to spend the night out, remember that your vehicle is probably your best shelter. In winter you will have to plan and improvise just to stay alive.

Don't struggle until you are exhausted. Stay with your vehicle to avoid becoming lost. Leave a downwind window open enough for oxygen to enter and run the engine and heater sparingly to conserve fuel. If it is snowing you could be there for a while. Exercise and move around to keep your circulation going. Keep a light burning to alert rescue crews and have someone watch for help at all times.

Advice for extreme emergencies

In extreme emergencies, your vehicle's headliner, seat covers, wall insulation or floor coverings can be used to keep warm. A fire for signalling or warmth can be started with engine oil from the dip stick or filter, or with fuel from the gas line or filter. A deflated spare tire makes a large black plume of smoke when burnt as a signal. Gasoline can be mixed with soil or sand and used for cooking or warmth. Even a battery, removed and wired, can start a fire by crossing the wires for a spark.

Wires from the electrical system can be used to make rope; so can strips of carpet or bedding. Emergency spotlights can be improvised by removing the headlights and rewiring them.

If you know you will have to spend the night out, avoid getting wet and exhausted. Your body will need reserve energy to keep you warm all night.

Though winter's main survival problem is cold, there are a few desert areas in B.C. that present special problems. Basically you should carry something to provide traction in sand, such as planks or several feet of mesh fencing, and you must remember to carry lots of water and to improvise shade if you become stuck.

All of this may make backroading sound risky and dangerous. It is not, but certain precautions must be taken. We have travelled thousands of miles on backroads; though we have been stuck many times, we have spent only one night out and only once did we need a winch. Fortunately, our preparedness that time included the company of a second vehicle equipped with a winch.

So take precautions. Be prepared, and all your backroading adventures will be stories to tell when you get home.

Appendix C
Backroads Ethics

As with most activities, particularly those involving the outdoors, there are certain ethics that accompany using the resource. Most of them involve courtesy and are common sense, though unfortunately they are not common enough. Keeping to the following few simple rules will not only make your journey safe and more enjoyable but will also leave the area in a condition attractive to others.

Don't drive on grass

Backroading involves vehicles that, misused, can cause severe damage to the environment. Any outdoor users can damage an area they pass through, but vehicles do it faster and easier. Whether you drive a passenger car, van, camper, 4x4, or a trailbike, you should stay on man-made roads. Travelling over grasslands, meadows or fields is not acceptable. The visual scars made by wheel tracks can last many years in fragile ecological systems.

Firewood should be gathered only from dead or fallen wood. Do not cut trees except in an absolute emergency.

Leave all gates as you find them. Do not cut fences or move barriers that may be holding stock.

Fishing and hunting rules

Anglers should take only what they can eat and, of course, must adhere to fishing regulations. Fishing also involves a set of ethics all its own and anglers should be aware of these.

Hunters should obey the ethics of their sport and not shoot from roads. Remember that some people find firearms and carcasses offensive. Treat your sport and the animals with the respect they deserve.

Respect history and nature

Historical sites may be looked at and photographed but not disturbed in any way. Antiques should be left. Removing old stoves, bottles, beds, barn boards or shakes is nothing more than stealing.

Wild flowers should be photographed but not picked. Trilliums, dogwood and rhododendron are protected by law in British Columbia. Such flowers do not last when picked, and in some cases the whole plant is killed when a single flower is disturbed.

Don't litter

Garbage and litter must be burned or carried out. Do not rely on local garbage cans; often they are not emptied for weeks or months. Equip yourself with large, strong plastic bags and have a place on your rig to stow garbage. Bottles and cans last indefinitely if thrown away. If you camp at a dirty site, clean it up. Do a little more to improve the place for the next person.

Toilets should be used where possible but otherwise a proper latrine should be dug. Do not just use the nearest tree. Carry a shovel.

Rules of the road

On the road remember that uphill traffic usually has the right of way. Watch for wide spots in the road and be prepared to move over or back up to make way for another vehicle. Move rocks or trees

Cattle don't always cross the road tidily. Approach with caution and be ready for emergencies.

from the road that may endanger other backroaders. Help anyone having trouble; not only is this good manners, but you may want help at the next mudhole.

If you become stuck and someone offers to tow you out remember that his rig, his expensive winch, even his fuel, is helping you out of a spot that you might have avoided if you were properly equipped. All of these things cost the other person money, so an offer of a few bucks is not out of line. Compare it with the cost of a tow truck from the nearest town or a cat from a logging show. At the very least, offer your thanks and return the favor to someone else in trouble.

Fire warning

Campfires must be drowned before you leave camp. They must be dead out. Report carelessness or forest fires to the local forest ranger. Be aware of any fire closures in your area. Remember that any Forest Service Officer has the authority to prohibit fires or order any person to extinguish a fire. Be extremely careful of all fires. Should you spot a forest fire, **dial '0' and ask for Zenith 5555**.

Respect private property

Go out of your way to respect private property. Always ask permission before travelling on private land.

Treat any areas you travel in as you would a park, or your backyard. Assume that you will be returning to the same place. Misuse and abuse often results in closures or restrictions of various kinds, either by private owners or government agencies or through pressure from various special-interest groups. This can be avoided by strict adherence to these few backroad ethics.

Appendix D
Map Information

Backroaders would be well advised to equip themselves with detailed maps in addition to those in this book. You may discover a road that we didn't cover, or want to know the name of that distant peak. Also, good maps will indicate contour lines and elevations, something that is not possible with our road maps.

A basic map for all people in British Columbia is the *British Columbia Recreational Atlas*, a 6½"x10½" book that covers the whole province at a scale of 1:600,000 or 1 cm to 6 km. The atlas shows all the administrative boundaries of the province's resource management regions as well as the wildlife management units, so it is particularly valuable to hunters and anglers.

Being a recreational atlas, it also shows the locations of all parks, recreation areas, nature conservancy areas, provincial and federal fishery facilities, spawning channels, recreational shellfish areas, launching ramps, historical monuments, ski areas, conservation officers, ranger stations, and all manner of roads and trails. One of the most useful features is the 9500-name index. Do you want to know where Noaxe or French Bar Creeks might be found? Just check the atlas index. There is no other such index for B.C., and that alone makes the purchase worth while.

The atlas, though, should not be used as the only source of information for backroading. The best maps are those produced by the provincial Ministry of Lands and Forests, Surveys and Mapping Branch, and available either from that branch in Victoria or most Government Agents. Depending on the region you plan to travel, several series are available with scales ranging from 1 inch to 4 miles, 1 inch to 2 miles and 1 inch to 1 mile. Not all scales are available for every region. These provincial maps also indicate the land status of surveyed lots.

A similar series of maps is available from the federal government through the Survey and Mapping Branch of the Department of Mines and Technical Surveys. One of the nice features of these series is that forested regions are colored green and cleared areas (which include alpine meadows and grasslands) are white. This makes it easy to get an idea of the terrain that a road passes through. These maps may be purchased from the department in Ottawa or from the local office in the Sun Tower Building (Beatty and Pender) in Vancouver.

Any of these maps will be of more use if you take some time to learn how to read them and translate the information. A few basic tools such as a pair of dividers, a rotary measuring scale, and a compass will greatly increase the map's use, as will a compass and altimeter in your vehicle. By taking a compass bearing on a couple of landmarks and adding the altitude you will be able to pinpoint your location on any map. Books and pamphlets are available on the basics of orienteering and it would be wise to spend a few hours learning the proper use of map and compass.

Detailed maps of individual roads and areas are often available from local tourist outlets, sporting-goods stores and the various logging and timber companies operating in the area. Some of these will indicate what type of vehicle the road is best suited for and, in the case of logging-company maps, when the road is open to the public. Check with the local or district offices of timber companies for this information.

Another group of maps of particular interest to recreationists is the new series being published by the Outdoor Recreation Council of B.C. Based on provincial topographical sheets, these maps include all the recreational points of interest in an area, including trails, camping sites, swimming, fishing, skiing and so on. At $3.95 they are good value. Look for them at most outdoor stores.

Appendix E

Annotated Bibliography

Since bibliographies have not been included in any of the other guidebooks in the 'Lower Mainland Backroads' series, this annotated bibliography includes reference books that would be of interest to backroaders in any of the areas covered by the four volumes. Not all books that outdoors folk carry should be reference books, so I have included a few that are good reading while you backroad. Many others could be added; these are a few that I have found useful or interesting over the years.

Akrigg, G.P.V. & Helen B. *1001 B.C. Place Names*; Discovery Press, Vancouver, 3rd edition, 1973.
Brief description in alphabetical order explaining the origins of many place names in the province, ranging from Abbotsford to Zymoetz. The mini-histories make interesting reading.
208 pp.

British Columbia Provincial Archives. *Our Native Peoples, Volume 3, Interior Salish*; Queen's Printer, Victoria, 1952.
Description of the way of life of the Indians of the Interior Plateau of British Columbia.
53 pp., photos, map.

British Columbia Provincial Museum.
— *The Mammals of British Columbia*
— *The Reptiles of British Columbia*
— *The Fresh Water Fishes of British Columbia*
— *The Birds of British Columbia* (9 volumes)
— *The Grasses of British Columbia*
— *The Ferns and Fern Allies of British Columbia*
— *Guide to Common Edible Plants of British Columbia*
— *Guide to Common Mushrooms of British Columbia*
— *Some Mosses of British Columbia;*
Queen's Printer, Victoria.
Part of a series of natural-history publications with scientific and local information relating to species of plants and wildlife found in British Columbia.

Brown, Annora. *Old Man's Garden*; Gray's Publishing Ltd., Sidney, 1970.
Folklore centring around wild plants, told in an engaging manner by a woman who heard many of the stories and legends from Indians and oldtimers.
268 pp., illustrations, index.

Cheadle, Walter B. *Cheadle's Journal of Trip Across Canada 1862-1863*; M.G. Hurtig Ltd., Edmonton, 1971.
An account of the travels of two men (sometimes called the first tourists) across the prairies, over the Yellowhead Pass, and through the colony of British Columbia. A great adventure. Gives good insight into early travelling conditions.
311 pp., illustrations, map.

Cherrington, John. *Mission on the Fraser*; Mitchell Press Ltd., Vancouver, 1974.
A history of Mission City from the founding of the mission by the Oblate Fathers up to the present day. Lots of interesting local detail.
238 pp., photos.

Chittenden, Newton H. *Travels in British Columbia*; Gordon Soules Book Publishers Ltd., Vancouver, 1984.
This new collection of Chittenden's writing, first published in 1882, gives an interesting perspective on British Columbia as it was a little over 100 years ago. As it tends to skim lightly over the area it is not an important book but certainly an interesting one.

Clark, Lewis J. *Wild Flowers of the Pacific Northwest*; Gray's Publishing Ltd., Sidney, 1976.
The most complete popular guide to wild flowers of B.C.

Includes botanical and historical information as well as color plates of many of the flowers. The large hardback volume is a little difficult to carry around but six field guides have been excerpted covering various biotic areas.
604 pp., photos, maps, bibliography, index.

Corner, John. *Pictographs in the Interior of British Columbia*; Wayside Press, Vernon, 1968.
A guide to pictographs or Indian rock paintings in the interior of the province. Includes directions for locating them. The book is now as hard to locate as the graphs and glyphs.
131 pp., illustrations, photos, maps, bibliography, index.

Decker, Frances — with Margaret Fougberg & Mary Ronayne. *Pemberton: The History of a Settlement*; Pemberton Pioneer Women, Pemberton, 1977.
A "homespun history" of the Pemberton area describing life with Indians and miners, then farmers and loggers.
348 pp., photos, map, bibliography, index.

Department of Forestry and Rural Development. *Native Trees of Canada*; Queen's Printer, Ottawa, 1966.
Guide to identifying trees. Includes physical descriptions and illustrative photos.
291 pp., photos, maps, index.

Department of Recreation and Conservation. *British Columbia Recreation Atlas*; Queen's Printer, Victoria, 1975.
Series of maps produced by the Department of Lands, Forests, and Water Resources, covering the entire province using a scale of 1:600,000. Gives details on Fish and Wildlife management units. The index of over 9000 place names makes this a valuable source book.
40 pp., maps, index.

Downs, Art. *Paddlewheels on the Frontier, Volume I*; Foremost Publishing Ltd., Surrey, 1971.
A photographic history of riverboats on the Lower Fraser River, the Cariboo and Central B.C., and the Skeena and Stikine Rivers. Good reading and interesting stories.
72 pp., photos.

Wagon Road North; Northwest Digest Ltd., Surrey, 1963.
A journey into the past with historic photos of the Cariboo Gold Rush and an explanatory text. Recommended reading.
80 pp., photos.

Duff, Wilson. *The Indian History of British Columbia, Volume I*;
Queen's Printer, Victoria, 1964.
Considers the impact of newcomers on the Indian way of life.
117 pp., photos, maps, bibliography.

Fraser, Simon. *Letters & Journals 1806-1808* (edited by W. Kaye
Lamb); MacMillan, Toronto, 1960.
The first documented ascent of the Fraser River, a journey
fraught with excitement and danger; also a personal view of the
Fraser country and its inhabitants at the time of first contact with
the white man.
292 pp., map, bibliography, index.

Freeman, Roger and David Thompson. *Exploring the Stein River
Valley*; Douglas and McIntyre, Vancouver, 1979.
It is hard to imagine a more complete guide to any area of the
province. Freeman and Thompson have detailed not only the
valley but all its approaches, so it becomes in effect a hiking
guide to the surrounding area. If you are going to the Stein, don't
go without it.

Godfrey, W. Earl. *The Birds of Canada*; Queen's Printer, Ottawa,
1966.
A complete guide to the birds found throughout Canada, with
color illustrations and details to aid in identification. A large
volume, not too convenient for field use.
428 pp., illustrations, maps, bibliography, index.

Harris, Lorraine. *Halfway to the Goldfields: A History of Lillooet*;
J.J. Douglas, North Vancouver, 1970.
The story of Lillooet from its beginnings as Cayoosh through the
gold rush days to the present. Stories of pioneer families.
102 pp., photos.

Hutchinson, Bruce. *The Fraser*; Clark Irwin & Co., Ltd., Toronto
and Vancouver, 1950.
Although somewhat dated, this is the only book that offers
anything like a complete story of the river. Good stories and
interesting tales.
336 pp., map, index.

Klassen, Agatha E. *Yarrow: A Portrait in Mosaic*; Agatha Klassen,
Yarrow, 1976.
Told through the experiences of the first Mennonite pioneers in
B.C., this book tells the story of the Sumas and Yarrow areas.
120 pp., photos.

Lyons, C.P. *Trees, Shrubs and Flowers to Know in British Columbia*; Dent, Toronto, 1952.
An early guide to the flora of British Columbia. Not as complete as some of the newer books, but still the most concise pocket guide to local plants.
194 pp., illustrations, index.

Macaree, David. *103 Hikes in South Western British Columbia*; Mountaineers, 1973.
A valuable trail guide for any hiker, though some details such as access points are out of date.
219 pp., photos, maps.

Marriott, Harry. *Cariboo Cowboy*; Gray's Publishing Ltd., Sidney, 1966.
The characters and cowboy philosophy of colorful days along the Cariboo Road.
207 pp.

Miyazaki, M. *My Sixty Years in Canada*; no publisher or date.
Memoirs of a pioneering Japanese physician in the Lillooet area.
137 pp.

Nelson, Ron, *...And When You Go Fishing...*; Oolichan Books, Lantzville, 1985.
Well known to BC OUTDOORS readers as a humorist and a fishing writer, Nelson has put together a collection of stories that, while ostensibly about fishing, go beyond and involve the reader in other things. Pick a story by a campfire with a mug of your favorite liquid and enjoy.
163 pp., illustrations.

Paterson, T.W. *British Columbia Ghost Town Series, Vol. 2, Lower Mainland*; Sunfire Publications, Langley, 1984.
One of many similar books from Paterson and Sunfire, this volume details old towns that fit closely with the area covered in *Bridge River Country*, Vol. 1 of the 'Lower Mainland Backroads' series. Some of the usefulness of this book is lost by the lack of an index, footnotes or bibliography.
160 pp., photos, maps.

Peterson Field Guide Series:
— *A Field Guide to Western Birds*
— *A Field Guide to Animal Tracks*
— *A Field Guide to Rocky Mountain Wild Flowers*
— *A Field Guide to Western Reptiles and Amphibians*

— *A Field Guide to the Insects of America North of Mexico*; Houghton Mifflin Co., Boston, various years.
A series of U.S. books that have become accepted as the standard against which all other field identification guides are measured.

Prante, Henry E. *Great Hunting Adventures*; Special Interest Publications, a division of Maclean Hunter Ltd., Vancouver, 1985.
Prante has been writing for B.C. magazines for decades and here collects his best hunting stories. Anyone who hunts (and many who don't) will enjoy an evening with Prante's book.
136 pp., illustrations.

Ramsey, Bruce. *Ghost Towns of British Columbia*; Mitchell Press Ltd., Vancouver, 1963.
This oft-reprinted, best-selling book about historic towns, forts and gold camps is still the best around, loaded with information of interest to backroaders and amateur historians.
226 pp., photos.

Sabina, Ann P. *Rock and Mineral Collecting in Canada, Volume 1*; Geological Survey of Canada, 1965.
A rather technical guide to some interesting geological sites and old mines with descriptions of rocks and minerals found.
147 pp., photos, maps, bibliography, index.

Shewchuk, Murphy. *Backroads Explorer, Vol. 1, Thompson Cariboo*; Special Interest Publications, a division of Maclean Hunter Ltd., Vancouver, 1985.
One of the 'Discovery Series' from SIP, this volume covers a wide territory — from Lytton in the south to Barkerville in the north. It is a mile-by-mile guide that will lead to many interesting areas in the back country.
170 pp., photos, maps, bibliography, index.

Underhill, J.E. *Wild Berries of the Pacific Northwest*; Hancock House, Saanichton, 1974.
A simple key to wild berries including recipes for food and wines.
128 pp., photos, bibliography, index.

Waar, Bob. *Off Road Handbook*; H.P. Books, Tucson, 1975.
A must for backroaders. Filled with information on tools, equipment, towing, winching, repairs, maintenance, and much more. Should be carried with you when backroading. Excellent photos and diagrams.
192 pp., photos, illustrations.

Wade, Mark S. *The Cariboo Road*; The Haunted Bookshop, Victoria, 1979.
The manuscript for this book was written in the 1920s and found 50 years later in an old trunk. Since published in a limited edition, it is a history of the Cariboo by someone who was there. It has no bibliography but offers a few footnotes.
264 pp., photos, fold-out map, index.

Waite, Don. *Tales of the Fraser Canyon*; Don Waite Publishing Ltd., Maple Ridge, 1974.
A guide to some of the colorful history along the Fraser between Hope and Lytton.
99 pp., photos, map, index.

Wright, Richard and Rochelle. *Canoe Routes: British Columbia*; Douglas and McIntyre, Vancouver, 1980.
A guide to more than 100 lakes and rivers for canoeists; many of the routes are in the Lower Mainland region. Sections on history, river classification, safety, equipment, first aid and ethics.
176 pp., photos, maps, bibliography, index.

Cariboo Mileposts; Mitchell Press Ltd., Vancouver, 1972. (Out of print.)
Points of interest along a famous road with information on road houses, history, natural history, side roads, fishing and esoterica. A mile-by-mile guide.
135 pp., color photos, bibliography, index.

British Columbia Cross-country Ski Routes; Douglas and McIntyre, Vancouver, 1983.
A revised edition of this popular guide adds 60 new and improved routes, making a total of more than 100 areas for cross-country skiers. Sections on safety, equipment, first aid, photography, and whom to contact for more information.
160 pp., photos, maps, bibliography, index.

Wright, Richard Thomas. *Overlanders*; Western Producer Prairie Books, Saskatoon, 1985.
With the discovery of gold on the Fraser in 1858 there was a rush to get to the new colony of British Columbia. Over the next five years more than 350 men and a few women trekked west across the plains and prairies. This is the story of their desperate adventures.
300 pp., photos, maps, bibliography, index.

Westering; Antonson Publishing, Surrey, 1978.
Essays of a writer; many of interest to outdoors people and lovers of wilderness. 174 pp.

Young, Cameron — with Bob Herger, Gunter Marx and Ken Seabrook. *The Forests of British Columbia*; Whitecap Books, North Vancouver, 1985.

Though a little pricey (at $39.95) for the average bookshelf, this is a valuable reference guide to the forests and biotic zones of the province. The informative text is illustrated with excellent photography that makes the book good value. Unfortunately, its usefulness for reference is hampered by the lack of an index.

192 pp., illustrations, maps, bibliography.

INDEX

155

S

U

V

W

T

Y

About the Author

Richard Thomas Wright is a well-known outdoors writer and photographer. He has explored much of this province by road and canoe and on cross-country skis, and enjoys backroading with his two sons. *The Junction Country* is an up-to-date revision of an earlier book entitled *Lower Mainland Backroads, Volume 3: Hope to Clinton*. The author's 16 books include three other guides to Lower Mainland explorations as well as others on the ski trails and canoe routes in this province. Richard Wright has also written more than 250 magazine articles. He now lives in Wells, B.C.

Look for these books of outdoor exploration and discovery to help you get the most from B.C.'s great outdoors!

DISCOVER BARKERVILLE
A Gold Rush Adventure
A Guide to the Town and its Time
by RICHARD THOMAS WRIGHT
One of British Columbia's best known outdoors writers recounts the exciting story of Barkerville, a town created by the 1858 Gold Rush. But unlike most of the boom towns of the Gold Rush years, Barkerville has survived into the twentieth century. This book looks at the origins of the town, its exciting history, and its restoration to the period of its 1870 heyday. Illustrated throughout with maps and fascinating archival photographs, this book is the perfect companion for your tour of this popular landmark and just plain good reading.

$6.95

THE BOWRON LAKES
A Year Round Guide
by RICHARD THOMAS WRIGHT
This is the first *complete* guide to the scenic Bowron Lakes chain — one of North America's most renowned canoe routes. And it describes the growing interest in cross-country skiing, that is making the area a year-round recreational attraction. Also included are interesting historical facts, commentaries on local personalities, and a valuable checklist of wildlife found in the region. Illustrated with black-and-white photographs and useful maps.

$7.95

BACKROADS EXPLORER
Volume 1 — Thompson-South Cariboo
by MURPHY SHEWCHUK

A book for everyone who has enjoyed Murphy Shewchuk's popular series in *BC OUTDOORS*. This comprehensive guide to the backroads of the Thompson-South Cariboo region is packed with information for the adventurous traveller; points of scenic and historical interest, recreational facilities, the best fishing areas, campsites and accommodation. Illustrated with black-and-white photographs and easy-to-follow maps, the kilometer-by-kilometer details will make every journey more rewarding.

$9.95

GREAT HUNTING ADVENTURES
by HENRY PRANTE

In this collection of exciting adventure stories, the author draws on his thirty years' experience of hunting all species in British Columbia. A great read, sure to stir the imagination of everyone who has ever hunted, or wished to hunt in B.C. Illustrated throughout with original line drawings.

$7.95

HOW TO HUNT DEER AND OTHER GAME
by LEE STRAIGHT

Packed with information on big (and smaller) game hunting in Northwestern U.S. and Western Canada. Species covered include deer, elk, moose, bear, wolf, cougar and more. Information on gun and ammo selection, proper gear, tracking, still-hunting and "driving" methods, and butchering game. Plus a special section on when and where to hunt.

$1.95

A CUTTHROAT COLLECTION
A Guide to Understanding and Catching the Mysterious Trout

The Cutthroat is being restored to fishable quantities by the Salmonid Enhancement Program. Until now, little has been written about this popular, but mysterious quarry. This collection fills the void. Noted experts, Bob Jones, Dave Stewart, Dave Elliott, Ron Nelson, John Massey and Karl Bruhn, pool their knowledge and experience to unravel the mysteries surrounding this elusive fish and help you understand, conserve, catch and cook it. Great reading for both fresh and saltwater fishermen.

$5.95

MAKE YOUR OWN FISHING TACKLE
by BOB JONES

Save money and have fun by putting your hands to work. Learn how to make your own tackle with Bob Jones. Sixteen information-packed chapters cover lures, spoons, spinners, wooden plugs, spinner baits, leadhead jigs, all kinds of molds, and more! Over 150 photographs and illustrations to guide you, plus tips on use and safety. Now you can equip your tackle box for pennies rather than dollars, so you'll be prepared to risk your tackle in the snag-filled waters you used to avoid — and where the fish are usually found. A small investment to make yourself a better angler!

$8.95

EXPLORING BRITISH COLUMBIA WATERWAYS
by DAVE STEWART

A mile-by-mile guide to the Okanagan, Shuswap and Kamloops regions, with detailed maps and scores of aerial photographs. This is for everyone interested in boating on the many lakes and rivers in B.C.'s southern interior. Includes information for canoeing and power boating, plus a special section of sailing Lake Okanagan.

$4.95

LOWER MAINLAND BACKROADS

This best-selling series covers the highways, byways and jeep tracks north of Vancouver, through the Lillooet district. Detailed maps and accurate directions ensure you get the most from your journey. Areas of scenic and historical interest, best fishing spots, campsites and recreational facilities are all included. Volume 1 has been completely revised and expanded by Richard Thomas Wright, and includes valuable information for mountain bikers. All books are illustrated with black and white photographs.

Volume 1 — Bridge River-Lillooet **$9.95**
Volume 2 — Fraser Valley **$4.95**
Volume 3 — Boston Bar-Clinton **$9.95**
Volume 4 — Garibaldi Region **$4.95**

CHARLIE WHITE'S 101 FISHING SECRETS

Charlie White is one of North America's most successful fishermen of all time. Now here's your opportunity to learn the secrets of his success! Charlie shares more than one hundred of his own special tricks to help improve your technique and increase your catch. No fisherman can pass this one up! Illustrated throughout with Nelson Dewey's distinctive cartoons and lots of helpful diagrams.

$6.95

LIVING OFF THE SEA
by CHARLIE WHITE

Here are detailed techniques for locating and catching crabs, prawn, shrimp, sole, cod and other bottomfish, oysters, clams and more! And how to clean, fillet, shuck — in fact everything you need to know to enjoy the freshest and tastiest seafood in the world. Illustrated with black-and-white photographs and lots of helpful diagrams.

$6.95

HOW TO COOK YOUR CATCH
by JEAN CHALLENGER

This useful little book shows you how to cook on board, at the cabin or campsite. Filled with shortcuts for preparing seafood for cooking, and delicious recipes for preparing dishes with simple camp utensils. Plus a special section on exotic seafoods.

$3.95

HOW TO CATCH SHELLFISH
by CHARLES WHITE
How, when and where to find and catch many forms of tasty shellfish. Oysters, clams, shrimp, mussels, limpets and more. Learn the easiest way to shuck oysters; the best equipment for clamming and shrimping; when not to eat certain shellfish. Know what to eat and what to discard. Discover how to outrace a razor clam. A delightful book chockfull of useful information. Illustrated. *Newly revised.*

$3.95

HOW TO CATCH CRABS
by CAPTAIN CRABWELLE
Now in its seventh printing, with revisions showing the latest crabbing techniques. This little book shows you how to catch crabs with traps, scoops, and rings; where and when to set traps; the best baits to use. It includes a detailed description of an easier, improved method of cleaning, cooking and shelling the meat. It's a great book, crammed with everything you need to know about catching crabs.

$3.50

WHERE TO FIND SALMON
Vancouver Island
by ALEC MERRIMAN
The catch dates and locations of more than 75,000 salmon caught in the season-long *King Fisherman* contest are combined with on-the-spot research, first-hand reports and local knowledge. Plus detailed maps of the "hot spots" and convenient charts let you know when and where the runs arrive in each area — so you can plan your fishing trips accordingly. Fishermen using this information have found the salmon showing up right on schedule!

$4.95

HOW TO CATCH SALMON —
ADVANCED TECHNIQUES
by CHARLES WHITE

The most comprehensive salmon fishing book available! Over 250 pages crammed full with how-to tips and easy-to-follow diagrams to help you catch more salmon. Covers all popular methods — downrigger techniques, mooching, trolling with bait, tricks with spoons and plugs. You'll find tips for river mouth fishing, catching giant tyees, winter fishing, secrets of dodger and flasher fishing, Buzz Bombs, Deadly Dicks, Sneaks and other casting lures — and much more!

$6.95

HOW TO CATCH SALMON —
BASIC FUNDAMENTALS
by CHARLES WHITE

This is the most popular salmon fishing book ever written! Here's the basic information you need for successful fishing: trolling patterns, rigging tackle, how to play and net your fish, downriggers — and where to find fish! Also included is valuable Fisheries Department information on the most productive lures, proper depths to fish and salmon habit patterns. This is *the* basic book on salmon fishing in the North Pacific and has now been expanded to include a section on the Great Lakes as well. Illustrated throughout.

$4.95

BOOK ORDER FORM

To: **Outdoors**
202-1132 Hamilton Street,
Vancouver, B.C. V6B 2S2

Please send me the following books:

HOW TO CATCH SALMON
  — Advanced Techniques   # 0085 _____ at $6.95 $_____

HOW TO CATCH SALMON
  — Basic Fundamentals   # 0086 _____ at $4.95 $_____

HOW TO CATCH STEELHEAD   # 0082 _____ at $2.95 $_____

HOW TO CATCH TROUT   # 0083 _____ at $3.95 $_____

HOW TO FISH WITH
    BUCKTAILS & HOOCHIES   # 0087 _____ at $2.95 $_____

HOW TO CATCH SHELLFISH   # 0090 _____ at $3.95 $_____

HOW TO CATCH CRABS   # 0091 _____ at $3.50 $_____

WHERE TO FIND SALMON   # 0084 _____ at $4.95 $_____

DRIFTFISHING TECHNIQUES   # 0088 _____ at $5.95 $_____

HOW TO CATCH BOTTOMFISH   # 0089 _____ at $3.95 $_____

HOW TO FISH WITH
    DODGERS & FLASHERS   # 0093 _____ at $2.95 $_____

A CUTTHROAT COLLECTION   # 0116 _____ at $5.95 $_____

MAKE YOUR OWN FISHING TACKLE
  — Volume I   # 0128 _____ at $8.95 $_____

CHARLIE WHITE'S
    101 FISHING SECRETS   # 0141 _____ at $6.95 $_____

LIVING OFF THE SEA   # 0142 _____ at $6.95 $_____

HOW TO COOK YOUR CATCH   # 0095 _____ at $3.95 $_____

DISCOVER BARKERVILLE   # 0115 _____ at $6.95 $_____

BOWRON LAKES   # 0140 _____ at $7.95 $_____

                           TOTAL PAGE 1 $_____

TOTAL PAGE 1 $_____

THE BEST OF B.C.'s
HIKING TRAILS   #0144 _____ at $9.95 $_____

PRINCE GEORGE BACKROADS   # 0102 _____ at $4.95 $_____

OUTDOORS WITH
    ALEC MERRIMAN   # 0105 _____ at $3.95 $_____

EXPLORING BRITISH COLUMBIA
    WATERWAYS   # 0103 _____ at $4.95 $_____

LOWER MAINLAND BACKROADS
—Volume 1 - Garibaldi to Lillooet #0096 _____ at $9.95 $_____
—Volume 2 - Fraser Valley   #0097 _____ at $4.95 $_____
—Volume 3 - Boston Bar to
        Clinton   #0098 _____ at $9.95 $_____
—Volume 4 - Garibaldi Region   #0099 _____ at $4.95 $_____
BACKROADS EXPLORER   #0143 _____ at $9.95 $_____
- Thompson-Cariboo
GREAT HUNTING ADVENTURES # 0139 _____ at $7.95 $_____

HOW TO HUNT DEER AND
    OTHER GAME   # 0106 _____ at $1.95 $_____

HOW TO SKI CROSS-COUNTRY # 0125 _____ at $5.95 $_____

HOW TO SKI TELEMARK   # 0124 _____ at $5.95 $_____

MARINE PARKS OF B.C.   # 0148 _____ at $16.95 $_____
        Sub Total $_____
        Postage and handling (up to 4 books
        50¢ per book, 5 or more 35¢ a book) $_____
                TOTAL $_____

☐ My cheque for $_____ is enclosed
☐ Visa   ☐ MasterCard

_____
CREDIT CARD NUMBER   EXPIRY DATE

_____
SIGNATURE

_____
NAME (PLEASE PRINT)

_____
ADDRESS

_____
CITY   PROVINCE   POSTAL CODE
ALL PRICES QUOTED ARE CURRENT AT TIME OF GOING TO PRESS.
HOWEVER, AS BOOKS ARE REPRINTED, PRICES MAY CHANGE.